Natasha,

I appreciate

feedback you

have on the book.

for taking the time you bot.

All the best to you bot.

personally and professionally!

Спасибо Большое!

Yours,

Frank

SEVEN BILLION BANKS

HOW A PERSONALIZED BANKING EXPERIENCE WILL SAVE THE INDUSTRY

BY FRANK H BRIA

Get additional information and research at

FrankBria.com

DEDICATION

This book is a product of both my experiences as well as the inspiration and encouragment of many of my colleagues. From industry professionals I have the pleasure of working with to analysts who cover the industry, they have all been a part of encouraging me to write a book what I have been sharing with audiences small and large for years.

A special thank you goes to Dr. David Whiting who reviewed some of my technical content to make sure I didn't say anything too stupid.

I wrote this book for my best friend, James. Only so he would stop telling me I never finish anything.

But mostly, I wrote this book for my wife and daughters who bring meaning and purpose to my life. No, they probably don't care too much about the future of banking, but they support me in all that I do. Even when doing that meant that I was half way around the world or didn't get to see them as often as I wanted.

They never complained. They all just cheered me on. Thank you.

WHY I WROTE THIS BOOK

My goal is to change the banking industry forever by encouraging banks to focus on improving the customer experience.

Based on how banks have been reacting to the most recent crisis, I truly believe that the banking industry is on the path to self-destruction, or at the very least, it is likely to be gobbled up by alternative players who do it better. And if this happens, isn't that the same thing? We could be beat at our own game by players like Paypal, Google, and Amazon— all are in the financial services industry already.

The public is best served by a prolific and technologically savvy banking industry in tune with the public's needs.

Knowing the needs of your customers isn't a requirement for opening a bank, but it's sure hard to keep one open when you don't.

WHY YOU SHOULD READ THIS BOOK

I have spent almost twenty years working in or for banks around the world. My primary focus has been leveraging data and analytics to improve both performance and customer experience. I have seen patterns emerge in how banks act. Some of those patterns hurt the industry while it tries to grow and transform itself. I want to share those observations with you.

If you feel that the banking industry doesn't need to change and will survive all alternative players nudging their way into the industry today, then we probably aren't going to agree on much in this book.

If, however, you are looking for a vision of the future of banking and want to know how to get there, this book is for you.

I address the big questions: who, what, where, when, and why of banking in the future. And I provide a plan for how to get there.

The book is split into five major components. They revolve around the following questions:

1. Why should banks change?
2. Where should banks go and when should they engage with the customer?
3. What should banks do?
4. Who should banks be?
5. How can banks get there?

I like to draw analogies to other industries because they have solved some of these problems that banking is wrestling with today. Also, so much of the future solution in banking revolves around analytics. Because that's a pet topic of mine, we'll spend a bit of time talking about data and advanced statistical modeling.

Don't worry. It won't be a math class. More like a philosophy class.

TABLE OF CONTENTS

Dedication 2

Why I Wrote This Book 3

Why You Should Read This Book 4

Part I. Why Should Banking Change? 9

    Chapter 1. The Case for Personalization 10

        Act Now 11

    Chapter 2. The Banks of the Future........................ 14

        Mobile Banking... 14

        Next Best Action 15

        Innovative Financial Products............................... 16

        1 + 1 + 1 = 7 Billion... 17

Part II. Where Should Banking Go (and When)? 19

    Chapter 3. Mobile Banking 21

        Push 22

        Pull 26

        Orchestration.. 29

    Chapter 4. Online Banking vs. Mobile Banking 34

        Decision-Oriented PFM 35

        The Online Contact Center 39

        What About the Tablet? 40

    Chapter 5. Old School Banking Channels 43

        The New Branch 44

        The New Contact Center 47

The New ATM 51

Part III. What Should Banks Do? 55

Chapter 6. Next Best Action in Marketing, Bundling, and Pricing
.... 57

Marketing 57

Bundling 61

Pricing 65

Chapter 7. Next Best Action in Servicing, Retention, and Collections
.... 73

Servicing 74

Retention 77

Collections 80

Chapter 8. The Foundation of Next Best Action: Data, Metrics, and
Models 92

Data 93

Metrics 99

Models 102

Chapter 9. The Execution of Next Best Action: The Decisions   116

The Trigger 117

The Decision Variable 119

The Objective 122

The Business Rules 125

An Optimal Decisioning System 128

Chapter 10. Examples of Optimal Decision-Making 130

Marketing 130

Pricing 132

Servicing 133

Retention 135

Collections 136

Enterprise Next Best Action........................... 138

Part IV: Who Should Banks Be? 141

Chapter 11. Unmet Customer Needs 143

Making Banking Clear and Simple 144

Helping Customers Make Better Decisions 153

Becoming an Advocate When Things Go Wrong 162

Chapter 12. Creating Financial Products of the Future

....168

Not Invented Here (in the Western Hemisphere)169

Meeting Those Unmet Needs........................... 170

Agile Banking 174

Part V: How Can Banks Get There? 179

Chapter 13. Regulatory and Compliance Impact.... 180

Not Taking Advantage of Customers................. 180

Not Letting Bad Things Happen.................... 183

Not Putting the Bank At Risk 185

Chapter 14. Planning the Vision 190

Get your "House in Order" 190

Improve Today.................................. 193

Create New Product 197

Turn Outward 198

Seven Billion Banks............................. 200

About The Author................................. 202

One Last Thing... 204

PART I. WHY SHOULD BANKING CHANGE?

Let's face it; the business model of banking is broken. This is evident in the decrease of customer trust, increased need for government regulation, more people opting out of the traditional banking system, and the appearance of alternative financial providers. When you consider the increasing reliance on fee income and the increased regulation of fees in different marketplaces, there's already a bit of a problem. Add the competition coming in from new players in the marketplace and it spells plain, bad news for the industry that's been felt over the last several years.

This section will answer the following questions:

- Why is the industry broken?
- What is the formula for a successful banking industry?

CHAPTER 1. THE CASE FOR PERSONALIZATION

The core value proposition that bankers try to execute with their customers is changing; no longer are banks clinging to the idea of simply moving money around from place to place.

This leads to a question: what should the banking value proposition be? Why would a personalized banking experience be the answer to that question? Because there are few levers left that bankers have to pull. From an income statement perspective, you've got expenses and revenue, the only two things you can really move. So on the expense side, the fixed expenses are all about controlling costs, and banks have pretty much milked out all of the opportunity in saving costs.

There are variable expenses that are both uncontrollable and macroeconomic in nature. And of course, there's nothing we can do about those. The controllable variable costs have led banks to make decisions which force them to take on less risk or provide fewer services, neither of which is a particularly palatable solution to the problem.

So we move over to the revenue side of the equation and there's non-interest income and interest income. The non-interest income is the fees, and that's essentially a difficult proposition because of regulatory guidance and frankly customer acceptance, and so we move to pricing.

There are really two models of pricing that a bank could take, pricing services as a commodity, and we've seen that in the past where there have been billboards for banks that talk about their freer-than-free checking accounts. I think that's a road that no one wants to go down. And so it leaves us with a value-based pricing methodology, but that is contingent upon creating the right value proposition.

Whatever the banking industry is doing today, it's not working. Only 19% of consumers in the four largest Western economies feel really valued by their bank. Banking customers consistently demand a personalized experience on their terms. 72% of consumers want to customize the format of the information that they receive from the banks, and 74% want to select the time that information is delivered.[1]

And so it becomes clear that we either have to develop micro-segmentation and focus on a niche market, such as small banks and credit unions can do, or if we want to create a large, scalable institution, we have to a create a value proposition that's going to be unique for each individual, and that requires a massive change in how we do business.

Act Now

Banks need to act now in order to stave off problems. Take a classic example of competing with an alternative player, Blockbuster versus Netflix. If you draw a picture of the ever-increasing number of Netflix subscribers on one axis and you look

---

[1] "The end of banking autocracy," Research, Ipsos Mori commissioned by GMC Software, November 2013. Consumers in US, UK, France, and Germany.

at the ever-declining Blockbuster share price on the axis (see Figure 1), you find that the two are inversely related to each other. And over time, as Netflix continued to get more and more subscribers, Blockbuster's share price dropped. There are really three sections of time, of what happened in that situation.

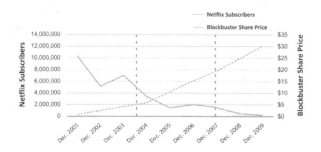

Figure 1. Blockbuster Stock Prices vs. Netflix Subscribers 2001 - 2009

Until about 2004, Blockbuster pretty much ignored Netflix as a competitor. They saw them as an outside force; they weren't serious, so there was nothing really to worry about. Between 2005 and the end of 2007, Blockbuster recognized that there was a serious problem. Instead of doing something about it, they blamed their systems which were unable to create new product or personalize recommendations – in other words, their legacy systems. So they used that excuse to be a follower of this new business model, rather than leading out.

And then right after 2008, Blockbuster essentially went out of business and Netflix took off as the new provider for video entertainment in the United States. Even though Blockbuster tried desperately at that point to get back on top, there was basically nothing they could do.

12

The lesson here is that even though legacy systems are problematic to making a change, it can no longer be an excuse to be a follower, because we will be out of business.

CHAPTER 2. THE BANKS OF THE FUTURE

I believe the bank of the future will be customized to each individual customer, all approximately seven billion of them.

A successful bank will be built around these three pillars which I will discuss in detail:

1. Mobile Banking
2. Next Best Action
3. Innovative Financial Products

MOBILE BANKING

I want to be clear on definitions here.

By mobile banking, I do not mean banking apps on smart phones. I'm referring to the concept that the bank needs to go where the customers are. Today that may be with a smart phone. Tomorrow who knows what that will be?

Rather than trying to make technology predictions about wearable devices or glasses or implants, I'd rather discuss the philosophy of being a bank "on the go." To me, it is much more important to discuss being where the customer is at all times and engaging when it is meaningful, than to devolve into a debate about native mobile apps versus responsive web design.

Thus, the only two important questions here are *where* the customer is and *when* he will have a need.

NEXT BEST ACTION

Next best action is a technology that allows a company to choose the next thing they do for their customers. This information is based on the latest data generated by the bank or received from the customer and maximizes the lifetime value of that customer, subject to the goals of the organization.

Similar to the previous section, I want to clarify what I am *not* referring to here. I am not discussing next best offer, which is a similar concept dedicated to finding the next thing the bank should sell to the customer. Next best offer is built on the assumption that the bank should always be selling. It's as if the bank believes the only thing that increases customer value is the acquisition of a new product.

I disagree with that assumption.

Bankers spend far too much time selling something new instead of maximizing what they have. While it is true that sometimes it is best to sell, history—and intuition—tells us that these moments are few and far between.

The reason bankers constantly sell is because they don't know when those moments will arrive. In other words, they sell all the time because they're not informed about the needs of our customers and when they will arise.

Sounds like a personal problem.

So why foist an "always be selling" attitude just because bankers don't know what their customers want and when they'll want it?

Let's solve that problem first.

Now your response might be that next best offer is still useful, but only when bankers choose to sell. That's closer to the truth, but banks spend almost no time trying to figure out what to do in between those moments.

And frankly, that's where the value is.

INNOVATIVE FINANCIAL PRODUCTS

Again, I want to be clear what I am *not* talking about.

When I describe innovative financial products, I am not referring to the brainchild of MBA graduates focused in mathematical finance that find a new way to hedge the risk and push it off onto some other third party. I think we've all had enough of those kinds of products.

What's fundamentally wrong with that philosophy is that it designs products from the perspective of the bank rather than the customer. It will be a mammoth shift in strategy for a bank to start designing products with the goal of maximizing the lifetime value of the customer rather than cost savings.

That's not to say bank profit isn't paramount. Of course it is. Without shareholder value there is no corporation.

My contention, however, is that shareholder value is best built by building customer value. When we've done that well in the past, we've been incredibly successful.

Innovative financial products need to be focused on meeting current unmet needs of our customers. Part of the crisis of trust that has emerged over the last several years in the industry is due to the lack of a coherent business model the customer can identify with. Because the customer sees the bank aligning *against* himself, anytime a trade-off needs to be made in a way that negatively impacts the customer, it is seen with anger and mistrust.

Partnering with the customer would change that dynamic.

1 + 1 + 1 = 7 BILLION

Together these three pillars (mobile baking, next best action, and innovative financial products) make a powerful combination. Banks are able to become the customized, personalized bank for each and every one of our customers.

The bank is personalized in a very real way. Being on the go—or "in your pocket"—based on today's technology, allows us to be a "real-time" bank. The bank gathers data, makes assessments of need, and immediately responds.

No need to go into a branch to get advice or do a transaction or even to be sold something. It's all happening right now.

And since the bank now knows exactly what to do and how to engage with each individual customer, the experience is unique. No two customers will have the same set of offers, reactions, communications, and even financial products. Nor should they.

Finally, the innovative financial products of the future will reflect the individual nature of the customer, as well as the new data-centric capability of next best action. That will make the financial product of the future feel more like a custom-tailored experience, rather than an "off the shelf" offering.

And the sad truth is that the banking industry is just not there yet. Matthew Lifshotz, Director of Business Development for Choice Financial Solutions summed it up nicely:

"As customers have grown accustomed to personalized solutions in other industries, the demand has begun to receive the same attention from their financial services providers. With all the innovation in other sectors, the financial world still has a long way to catch up." [2]

But the benefits are there. In the same article, Mr. Lifshotz continues:

"In market research conducted by GfK which obtained results from consumers with over $10,000 in deposits, over 40% surveyed said they would be more included to continue their relationship with their primary bank if they offered products where the economics of the product could be personalized." [3]

There are certainly technology barriers that keep the banking industry from offering these personalized economics, but in many cases, the barrier is one of vision. The industry needs to see that personalization is its ticket off this self-destructive spiral down to sameness and mediocrity. That conveyor belt just leads to being beat by other players who are willing to be smart and fast.

---

[2] "It's Time for Personalization in Financial Services," Matthew Lifshotz, The Financial Brand, January, 17, 2014.
[3] Ibid

Part II. Where Should Banking Go (and When)?

Let's take the three pillars, mobile banking, next best action, and innovative financial products, and dig into them a little.

The bank of the future must be mobile. But it's not enough to say that. Bankers also have to describe what they do with all the existing interaction points.

Bankers are hampered a bit in the industry by talking about "channels." Those may in fact be our current interaction points, but that term gives the false impression that each channel is somehow an independent unit of the bank.

I'd rather discuss the interfaces with the bank because I think that's more accurate. Each interface is different, but not equal—much less independent.

This section will address those interfaces and answer these questions:

- What does "mobile banking" mean?

- What's the difference between a mobile banking experience and an online banking experience?
- What should be done with all those other interfaces with the bank, such as the branch, contact center, and ATM?

CHAPTER 3. MOBILE BANKING

As I mentioned earlier, I'm not talking about smart phones. Instead, I want to define what a successful "on the go" experience should look like.

Whatever device happens to be popular at the time, it's clear that we are a mobile people. We have long since crossed the threshold of being "always on," for good or for bad. Of course, it's left to each individual to manage that sense of connectedness, but as an industry, banking must respond to their customers' need for information at all times.

I argue that whatever device we have with us at all times becomes our main source for information. Just as banks have systems of record, for us, the mobile device is increasingly becoming our system of record.

Because we rely on our mobile devices to serve as a key source— if not *the* key source—of data, any successful mobile strategy needs to have three component parts: push, pull, and orchestration.

Push "pushes" alerts or information to the user in real-time in order to encourage some action. Pull means that the user initiates a connection, sends data, and requests information back. These two concepts are well known in mobile strategy.

Orchestration, however, is new. By orchestration, I mean that the mobile device is the central management vehicle for all interactions, virtual or in-person. I will discuss all three components in greater detail later in this section.

There is a much-discussed concept in banking called "omni-channel." Omni-channel allows the customers to interact with the bank in any method they choose; each interaction channel is synchronized with the others so that the movement across channels is seamless.

In this parlance, the mobile device should be the central director of the omni-channel experience. Because it is with us at all times (or almost all times), the mobile device is the perfect centralized conductor of the complex symphony that is omni-channel interaction.

Banks are making innovations in mobile banking applications along these lines. It's not a coincidence that the winner and honorable mention for BAI-Finacle Global Banking Innovation Award for Disruptive Business Model in 2013, Hana Bank and Jibun Bank both from South Korea, were recognized for their innovative mobile strategy. In both cases, the mobile device acted as the coordinator of banking services, providing information and assistance in real-time.

There is still progress to be made on time-sensitive and relevant push alerts, but this shows that the direction of mobile is central to the new banking platform.

PUSH

The concept of push makes mobile applications very powerful. It doesn't just wait on the user to make a request; it sends out a specific call-to-action to the user based on the user's context.

Chris Skinner, chairman of the Financial Services Club and CEO of Balatro Ltd., describes it as the "intellisensing bank:"[4]

> *This is the contextual bank that recognizes customers' needs in real-time as they connect with devices and embedded chips during their everyday lives. The bank then focuses on sensing what the customer needs as they make their digital movements and proactively delivers them marketing and advisory services to them in real-time.*

In a sense, that's what makes mobile so much better than online applications. An online application at a PC can only push when the user is at the computer. Since a mobile device is often with customers most of the time, these push alerts are much more useful.

Effective push alerts all comes down to context.

What do we mean by mobile push context? There are four categories of push context in the framework of a banking application: the bank context, the location context, the time context, and the user interaction context. I'll discuss each one.

The bank context is the information generated by data that resides in the bank. This data includes transactions and interactions. Essentially, the bank context is any data that can be generated by the bank alone and does not necessarily involve the mobile device.

This context is the most frequently used push alert. A bank, for example, may push an alert when the balance on an account is below a certain level as set by the customer. Or, a push alert is sent when a large transaction clears a credit card.

---

[4] "Transparency in Banking for 2014," Chris Skinner, BAI Banking Strategies, January 24, 2014

The bank context push alerts lets the customer know that something has happened that they may not be aware of. But the goal of a push alert is not simply to inform, but to encourage customer interaction.

In the case of a low balance, perhaps the customer should transfer funds. In the case of a large transaction, perhaps the customer should verify the purchase was initiated by him. In either case, it is the bank's responsibility to suggest a probable action based on the alert.

The next most popular context for push alerts is the location context. Many banks are experimenting with using geolocation information from the mobile device to push an alert based on where the customer is. For example, customers may get an alert when they are near a store where they have previously purchased items. It's even better when that store is a merchant of the bank, and the bank can receive the interchange fee from the use of a debit card and the merchant discount as well.

Here, it is clear that the push alert cannot just inform. It cannot simply tell customers that they are near a store; they probably know that already. But the alert needs to tell them they can get a discount, or that they may need to purchase groceries because the bank has analyzed such a purchase is probable and profitable.

Location context push alerts must encourage action of some kind. In turn, the mobile application or the bank's core systems need to record the result of that suggestion—whether successful or unsuccessful—so that the bank can improve its alerts in the future.

In case the push alert recommended a purchase, the core system needs to monitor purchases from that recommended merchant within a certain time frame to see if such an alert motivated action. In the case of a discount, the transactions may even track a monetary volume to see if the discount was used.

Another popular push alert is the time context alert. The time context alert pushes a recommended interaction based on a specific time frame—whether that's time of day, day of week, or number of days after some other event. In banking, this could easily be a reminder to pay bills or make a scheduled transfer of funds.

However, the time context alert can also remind the consumer that a scheduled or expected action did *not* occur within a specified time frame. For example, if the expected direct deposit of a paycheck did not occur within two days of the typical time, an alert would be sent.

These types of alerts traditionally have been requested by the customer. They set up specific things they would like to be warned about. But this is very limiting. The alert that an expected action did not occur is a rare event, and as such, the customer is unlikely to anticipate it. However, because it is a rare event, its impact is often quite high.

It is completely within the statistical ability of analytic teams to trace expected financial events and monitor when they do not occur. Banks do this already to prevent fraud, just backwards. They look for events that are out of the ordinary. They can simply take the same analytic models and turn them around: analyze the lack of transaction that would be expected.

Notifying a customer that they missed a paycheck, did not pay a bill, did not get a scheduled transfer, or otherwise had an unusual transaction pattern is a very high value offering. A push context of this type would elevate the value proposition of a mobile banking application or other SMS alert offerings.

Finally, the least used push context is the user interaction context. This context involves understanding how the customer is using their device at that moment. A customer may be using the device to scan a barcode for price shopping; they may be using the device to schedule an appointment with a realtor, or they may be using the device to search for car prices. In any of these cases, a targeted push alert to engage with the customer can be very valuable.

The biggest argument against this kind of interaction is data privacy. Consumers have indicated, however, that they see the sharing of data as a value exchange; when they receive something of value in return, they are more open to allowing this kind of data to be collected.

Data needs to be collected with permission, of course. Once the value proposition has been outlined, the customer can allow access to this information assuming the bank can provide sufficient value. That value is defined as the relevance of the interaction.

This comes down to the accuracy of modeling predictions. Banks need to invest the time and energy to find those interactions, which are predictive of profitable customer engagement. That will require testing and piloting of different ideas. But there is huge value in such an endeavor—mostly because no one is effectively operating in this space today.

PULL

Pull is the most common interaction in a mobile application. Here the customer initiates a request to the bank, and the bank processes the request and responds.

Customers initiate an interaction with the bank for two primary reasons: to request information or to complete a transaction of some kind. Fortunately, most banks do a good job in fulfilling these requests. In case yours does not, you need to play catch up. These are table stakes and cannot be ignored even today.

Many mobile banking applications, however, serve as a watered-down version of an online banking experience. That should not be the case. Every piece of information that a customer could request from the contact center should be available here. Should a user need to contact the bank, it needs to be one click away— whether by phone, voice over IP (VOIP), or chat.

A big anti-pattern in mobile applications is the separation of phone numbers from the phone application. Phone numbers should be clickable to access the dialing application of the device. In case the mobile device does not have phone capabilities or in the case of a request by the user, alternative connection should be made via web video or text chat. The customer should not have to copy and paste the phone number into the dialer, and heaven forbid the customer having to write the number down on paper because it's not clickable at all.

Often the excuse is made that contact center requests go down when the number is more difficult to access and interact with. This is a tautology. Of course, requests go down. Would you like them to go down to zero? There is no long-term business proposition built around customer friction. If yours is, change it or be beat by other players who figure out how to make the cost equation work out.

Of course, the easiest way to decrease contact center requests is to provide the data natively. More than just balance and transaction data, search is now considered key mobile functionality. Make your search functionality easy to access on a mobile device. Test calendar user interface (UI) components and drop-down lists for usability.

Completing transactions is an area where mobile banking applications still are inconsistent. Some institutions provide excellent capacity to complete all necessary transactions the customer would want while others simply provide a window into balances and provide limited transfer capabilities.

It's now considered standard to provide account-to-account transfers and mobile deposits. Bill payment is considered secondary, but shouldn't be. Mobile bill payment via camera input is a newer technology but has promise to increase bill payment adoption by lowering the upfront work necessary for setup.

Interactions that are currently not viewed as mobile interactions but could include starting transactions, which need to complete in another channel. Initiating an ATM or branch cash withdrawal could expedite the process. This initiation in the mobile channel and completion in another is the promise of omni-channel.

This omni-channel approach to mobile banking significantly increases the functionality of the mobile application. It opens the door to efficiency and customer satisfaction. But beyond simply providing functionality, the mobile application has much more untapped promise.

The biggest mistake most banks make in their mobile strategy is to satisfy pull requests and store no information about the transaction. The interaction history on a mobile application is a key source of data about how customers use banking services and in particular, how they define the value proposition from their perspective - not the bank's.

Let me be clear. Banks should store every request made through the mobile application and use that data as the source for predictive models on customer behavior and in modeling lifetime profitability.

The future, personalized bank will be centered on the mobile application. These interaction requests serve as the basis for the customer experience. If banks do not leverage this data, they are missing the customers' voices in describing how they want to interact with their bank and what they see its purpose is.

ORCHESTRATION

Given that mobile devices are so central to our daily living, it is natural that they become the customer's "system of record." More than being a central repository of information, the mobile device should actually direct engagement across the different channels a customer may engage. I call these "handshakes."

The easiest handshake to understand is the one between the mobile device and the online banking application. Since the online banking application will generally have all of the pull functionality from the mobile application, the handshake simply involves syncing the data between the two devices. This is generally accepted as a given, since both applications will pull from a real-time snapshot of the customer's profile.

The next handshake is the use of mobile to control the ATM experience. I'll discuss this in more detail in a couple of chapters, but it's important to think of the mobile device as directing action at the ATM.

Many banks, especially in Europe, are experimenting with the use of NFC and SMS code sending to eliminate the use of cards and PINs at ATMs. Not only does this allow a multifactor authentication security protocol, but it also provides quicker access to information at the ATM. For example, with a coordinated handshake between the mobile device and the ATM, no longer does a customer need to explicitly request their balance before making a withdrawal request. And, as will be discussed later, the ATM can provide value-added information about cash availability to the customer.

The handshakes become much more complex and interesting when they involve coordination between the mobile device and human interaction at the branch or contact center.

The most obvious handshake between the branch or contact center and a mobile device would include multifactor authentication. Instead of requesting ID or asking obscure security questions, the representative could simply request the time-sensitive token as pushed to the mobile device in order to authenticate the individual.

Beyond security is the true value of the mobile banking orchestration. Customers can initiate transaction on the mobile device and complete at the branch. For example, a customer could request a cash withdrawal, money order, or other complex financial transaction via the mobile device. This transaction could be queued up for completion at a particular time in the branch so that the customer can come in later at their convenience.

Queuing up transactions in advance, especially more complex ones has the advantage of allowing the branch and contact center to monitor and manage staffing levels. In addition, by completion authentication in advance, the transaction is much quicker and will result in a higher level of customer satisfaction.

In addition, because the mobile device is storing information about the request and the contact center or branch representative is notating completion of that transaction in the core system, data can be collected that will assess customer satisfaction and engagement. Although raw transaction data is currently stored in the core system, context of the transaction, such as customer need, timing, and satisfaction with service is almost never stored. The traditional excuse for not storing such information is that the core system is not designed for such interaction tracking, and redesigning the core system, or heaven forbid, core replacement is not cost effective.

This data, however, can be tracked if the mobile application serves as the nerve center for customer engagement. It is much easier to build these components into a new mobile application than it is to try to engineer them into the core system.

The mobile banking application, therefore, becomes the brain of the customer experience while the core system remains the financial storage system. This separation of purpose allows for agile development of a new customer experience while leaving the sensitive core system alone.

Mobile Banking Recap:

To summarize, any mobile banking infrastructure needs to support three components: push, pull, and orchestration.

Push alerts are built are four major context areas:

- Banking context, referring to information gained from data owned and stored by the bank (e.g. transaction, interactions, etc.)
- Location context, referring to geographic information as detected by the mobile device
- Timing context, referring to passage of time or specific time triggers pushed on a particular schedule
- User-interaction context, referring to the way the customer is using the mobile device at the moment

In each context area, the goal is for the bank to provide suggested actions—not just information—as a way of maximizing the customer's lifetime value. This key difference of action over information is the core of the future banking value proposition.

Pull is focused on information and transaction processing. Successful mobile experiences will expand the information available and connect directly to other channels, which can continue the availability of information. Mobile experiences that focus on a robust search functionality will reduce the drain on more expensive channels such as the contact center.

Transaction processing needs to focus not just on transaction that can be completed through the mobile channel, such as money transfers and mobile deposits, but also those that either replace or facilitate transactions that today only occur in other channels.

For example, mobile bill pay can move from an online only function to one, which utilizes the mobile device's camera to make payee setup much easier. In addition, some transactions can be started in the mobile channel and completed in person. Cash withdrawals or new account applications can begin on the device and end in person. This omni-channel experience can even serve to shorten lines within branches or hold times at contact centers.

Finally, the mobile application serves as the central nervous system of the customer experience. It has handshakes between other channels to coordinate and centralize interactions.

As the mobile application interacts with other system, it does so in two major areas: security and providing contextual data.

Security using mobile devices certainly centralizes around multifactor authentication, but includes other mobile technologies just as NFC.

Contextual data allows the mobile device to provide additional insight into the interaction in a way that would be either time consumer, insecure, or impossible in the other channel. For example, providing balance and cash flow projection information at the ATM is much more secure and efficient through the mobile device than on the ATM screen.

Handshakes between the mobile device and human interaction channels, such as the branch or contact center primarily serve two purposes. These handshakes can prearrange services so they can be provided in a more efficient and satisfying way. They can also serve as the information storage hub for all customer interactions so that the outcomes of each touch point are analyzed to make the experience better, but bypass typical frontline system, such as the core system or loan servicing system; this makes the storage and analysis of this data more cost effective and independent of costly core system upgrades or replacements.

Chapter 4. Online Banking vs. Mobile Banking

The traditional view is that mobile banking is a compact subset of the online experience. Because of the smaller form factor of today's smart phones and the idea that people have more time for analysis when they're sitting at a computer, the online banking application has become the smarter big brother of the mobile application.

I argue this is completely backwards.

Certainly form factor means that whatever is displayed on a mobile device needs to be more compact and consumable on the go than online banking applications. But let's look at it from the consumer's perspective. Where do I make most of my financial decisions?

Historically, online banking began as a support of other personal financial management (PFM) tools. People wanted to see their transaction history, balances, and perhaps download that information into another tool for financial management. This would all be done at a desk strewn with paper statements, receipts, and checkbook registers in order to reconcile the account and make sure people really understood where their money was going.

Those days are (almost) over.

Banks responded to that dynamic by creating more financial management tools inside the online banking applications. By including fancy charts and graphs, the hope was that people would go to their online banking site for PFM, rather than relying on third-party tools like Quicken or Mint.com.

But that just isn't happening.

The adoption rate of PFM is very low, and these tools still require a great deal of setup. If you're hyper detail-oriented, then you may invest the time to set up spending categories, budgets, and connect all of your financial accounts to download automatically into one system. But what consumers are telling banks is that they're not that hyper detail-oriented.

One reaction to this feedback is to make this financial reconciliation process simpler. But that just means the bank engages at the tail end of that process—after all the financial decisions have been made and the customers are now just getting around to seeing how bad of a mess they've made of it all.

So, where do I make my financial decisions? In "the field," so to speak. At stores, in the mall, when I shop, when I save. Our financial decisions are made daily as we go about our regular business.

If banks want to engage in financial decision-making, then the core function—the "smarter big brother," if you will— needs to travel with us.

The online banking experience may help us clean up the mess customers have made, but the mobile banking experience needs to help prevent them from making the mess in the first place. And that is a much more difficult proposition.

DECISION-ORIENTED PFM

PFM tools have been deployed by banks and outside vendors to try to fill a need for customers that are looking for a complete financial picture and guidance in their day-to-day money management. There is much discussion about PFM as the "killer banking app." The last several years has seen significant investment both within and outside of banks to develop these kinds of tools.

Adoption, however, has been lackluster. In 2012, an Aite Group survey[5] found that 58% of customers said they do not use PFM tools and have no plans to do so. Ron Shevlin, the author, cites survey results that show only 13% of those surveyed indicated that they wanted their bank involved in basic financial management.

To give you a sense of how bad the product fit is, back in 2013, analysts were discussing industry averages of adoption in the single digits. At the same time, a bank in Tennessee was lauded for their amazing 25% adoption rate of PFM. This seems like a poor showing and definitely not the adoption rate of the "killer app" promised by PFM vendors.

Could that be because consumers do not trust their financial institutions with their data? Possibly, although I think that is a temporary problem. Clearly, the industry has suffered a "black eye" over the 2008–2010 timeframe because of the financial crisis, but it hasn't always been that way.

I argue that consumers do not see banks as participating in day-to-day financial management because banks do not offer anything of value today in that regard.

---

[5] "Strategies for PFM Success," Ron Shevlin, Aite Group, 2012

PFM is generally centered around categorization and budgeting. Most consumers don't think this way about their finances. Consumers look at financial decisions on a case-by-case basis, and although they have general targets in their heads about what they can spend and cannot spend, they typically don't think of budget categories when evaluating a purchase.

The setup associated with the successful and effective use of PFM is a very high bar, beyond what most customers are willing to invest. I call this the "setup barrier," and it is unnecessary.

Leveraging data and analytics is the key to solving the setup barrier problem. By analyzing transaction history, a bank can easily identify key cash flow events: paychecks, rent, monthly credit card payments. You don't need a customer to identify them for you, much less categorize them.

Will you be right 100% all of the time? Of course not. But in some sense, who cares? They are still relevant cash flow events with some statistical and real-life meaning. Maybe you misread some major payment as the rent or mortgage. But if it occurs every month (like housing payments should), it is still an important cash flow event and should be tracked. The only thing you miss is its category. And as I've pointed out, most customers don't manage their funds that way.

Customers are much more interested in cash flow, overdrafting their accounts, making purchasing decisions, ensuring that they aren't being ripped off by debit or credit card transactions they haven't authorized, and other such non-category oriented items.

Right now, the market offers some of these services as niche financial management tools. No one has truly brought them together in one package, and banks certainly have not implemented the predictive, decision-oriented PFM mindset.

The theme should be clear by now. Information over action is the root cause of why PFM is not adding enough value for the customer today. PFM tools are meant to simply inform, not help people make better decisions about their money. Graphs and charts about how much money is being spent on entertainment versus electricity is nice, but what is a customer supposed to do about that? Spend more on electricity? Cut back on eating out?

Decision-oriented PFM is the answer. Let me define what I mean. Decision-oriented PFM is a financial management tool specifically engineered to help customers make financial decisions; it doesn't just give them information. The key characteristic of a decision-oriented PFM is that no data should be displayed that doesn't help a customer make a decision. And that decision should be able to be executed from the PFM tool. Otherwise, we have the "copy-paste" problem: where I have to manually move information from one application to another in order to act on it.

Clearly, this operates much more effectively when decision-oriented PFM is integrated into online banking applications. Why online and not mobile? Most often, long-term financial planning decisions are not made on the fly, but sitting at a desk in front of a computer. Thus the online channel is a natural fit. However, PFM in the mobile channel can also be effective, especially when the decisions made come with mobile context—the kinds we discussed in the last chapter.

But didn't survey results show that customers don't want their bank involved? Yes, however, a May 2014 BankChoice Monitor survey fielded by Novantas[6] indicated that of those customers currently using PFM tools, over 40% of them indicated they would prefer to use the tools on the bank's own website.

This squares the circle. It demonstrates that customers inherently want their bank to be involved, once they see the value proposition. Until then, it's just another useless trinket the bank is trying to sell.

THE ONLINE CONTACT CENTER

Once a customer sits down at a computer with an Internet connection, the ways a bank can communicate with him expands significantly. As an industry, the bank has specifically adopted the term "contact center" to replace the old "call center" as recognition of this fact.

Many banks now provide online chat through their online banking applications. This integration allows their customers to speak to representatives about sensitive account-related items that would otherwise require authentication. Why pick up the phone and re-authenticate, when you've already done so via the web?

In 2013, eDigital's Customer Service Benchmark[7] reported customer satisfaction statistics on various contact methods. A full 73% of users indicated that they were happy with live chat as a support experience. Compare those statistics with only 44% of phone support. And although not specific to banking, these general trends are about customers' preferences.

Add to that chat functionality video conferencing, and banks can significantly adjust the costs associated with staffing their centers.

---

[6] "Gen Y Hopes Their Next Bank Helps Them Budget Better," Rob Rubin, The Financial Brand, thefinancialbrand.com, May 20, 2014
[7] Customer Service Benchmark Study, eDigitalResearch, 2013

Perhaps our customers don't have or don't want to use their webcams. That's okay. Visual cues—even if one-way—can make a huge impact on the relationship and satisfaction level of the interaction.

There are a number of tools integrating websites into live contact centers. These should be looked at not just from a cost-savings perspective, but also from a customer-satisfaction perspective. This kind of integration qualifies as omni-channel since the customer starts in the online channel and continues the interaction live.

Many of these tools "push" the interaction to the customer instead of just waiting for the customer to request one. Often, this is done in sales-related situations, where customers are clearly looking to make a purchase based on their clickstream history and where they are spending their time.

There certainly is room for this kind of interaction on our websites. In order to avoid being seen as "pushy" and an interruption, however, clickstream analysis should be used to find those trigger moment most likely to result in a positive interaction. The standard practice is for implementation consultants or—even worse—application developers to choose which triggers are relevant and should result in a contact offer. Don't fall victim to this trap. If this is done, at the very least the data and success of each contact request should be collected in order to refine the efforts. In short, use data to find the right opportunities.

WHAT ABOUT THE TABLET?

Many readers have probably wondered where the tablet discussion is hidden. I've attended several conferences with sessions debating tablet vs. mobile. I find most of these discussions less than helpful.

It's true that the tablet offers a different form factor than a mobile device or computer. User experience designers should take that into consideration when designing UI components and outlining use cases. Even time of day varies by device.

A UK-based data consultancy called comScore published a time-of-day study[8] based on different device usage. It showed that UK users on a typical Monday preferred mobile phone in the morning, PCs during work hours, and tablets at night. (See Figure 2.)

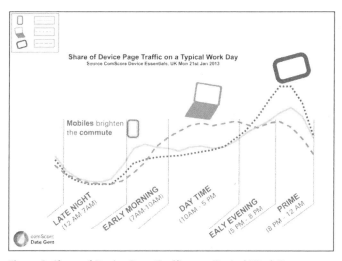

Figure 2. Share of Device Page Traffic on a Typical Work Day

This usage pattern indicates that there are two dimensions to the tablet discussion. The obvious one is form factor. The tablet's relatively larger screen and user orientation allow for different UI experiences and potentially more information. It is important,

---

[8] "An Average Monday in the UK: PCs for Lunch, Tablets for Dinner," comScore, comscoredatamine.com, February 18, 2013

however, to remember that mobile phone screens are getting larger and larger. This change makes the form factor argument less powerful.

The second dimension, which is much more relevant even with changes in form factor, is use context. Evening usage is a mobile time context, as discussed in the chapter on mobile banking. Is the answer to provide special feature function on a tablet application because the tablet is uniquely an evening-oriented device? Or is it more effective to think about use cases in context of the time of day? If so, it becomes clear that whatever the strategy, a time-sensitive user experience will outlast whatever the device du jour happens to be. Today it's tablet. Tomorrow it may be glasses or watches. But the use context will change, and instead of thinking about each device as its own "channel," banks should be thinking in terms of use context and adapting appropriately.

CHAPTER 5. OLD SCHOOL BANKING CHANNELS

If you want to make a good living as a banking expert, predict the death of branches. It seems to be the oldest sport among those who do this sort of thing.

No matter how much these experts declare the branch dead, it lives on still. I won't join that chorus. Instead, I'll declare the branch *as we know it* dead. Or at least, it's a dead man walking. Similarly, many of the traditional bank channels will also have to change in this new banking environment.

It is a bit odd that the place most consumers (especially younger ones) say they hate going is the same place the banking industry spends billions of dollars a year to make them want to go. In addition, with the increase in mobile banking, branch visits are declining. In a recent study, mobile banking users reported visiting their branch 39% fewer times than before.[9]

In some sense, it feels a bit like a losing battle. I guess there are two ways to deal with a losing battle. One is to fight harder, which is what the "branch of the future" tries to do. With the use of tablet and fancy technology, it tries to make the branch "fun" and "cool."

But I think the other way is inevitable. Retreat. Stop making consumers go to the branch.

---

[9] "AlixPartners Mobile Financial Services Tracking Study," AlixPartners, March 2014.

There are several protests from the industry about how the branch channel is the most expensive, but it's also the one channel that offers all the services, all the touch points. If expenses are going to be lowered, the branch needs to be a limited function channel.

Now many argue that the reason the branch never dies is because consumers tell us time and time again that they pick a bank because of branch location. And that is true. For now. This is why I would never forecast the death of the branch.

But we don't have to willingly participate in this ongoing madness.

So I'll make a prediction. My guess is that the power of the branch as a local draw for selecting banking services would still be there even if the branch were to become a limited function channel. The psychology of the building would serve as the draw, as long as the functions were easily obtained in other, potentially cost-saving or—and this is the important part—more convenient ways.

THE NEW BRANCH

There is only one reason to enter a physical building and talk to another human being: you need to enter a physical building to talk to another human being.

I know that sounds obvious, but it should be the guiding principle behind the branch offering. Unless you can justify why a human being needs to be involved in the process, it shouldn't be in the branch.

But you say your branches have kiosks for customers to get what they want without talking to anyone? That's just a bunch of ATMs under one roof. That's not a branch. We'll deal with ATMs later, but I'm talking specifically about the things banks make people do in person, even if they don't want to.

Those things include: account opening, signing documents, getting money orders, cashing checks, etc. None of these things need to involve a branch.

Depending on the country you're operating in, regulation may require some in-person transactions. Be creative. That may not mean the bank has to build a large building and staff it all the time.

It's vogue these days to call our branches "sales centers." That reflects the idea that sales occur best in person and well, what are you doing with all those people in the branch?

I want to challenge that notion slightly.

Sales do not necessarily occur best in person. Ask Amazon. Financial services sales occur best in person only because they are so bad in all our other channels. That's not the measuring stick that should be used. Banks hire (relatively) expensive sales agents expecting them to figure out the need of customers, and then the banks make the product selection process so unruly that it requires an adventure guide to help them through it.

Technology solves both of those dilemmas.

The branch is where the three basic mistakes of being too impersonal, too late, and too short sighted are made.

The branch has access only to the models that have been built in the analytic department. True, the branch staff should have the skills to sense when things have changed, but how many of the bank's staff can truly do that?

Our models are stale, for sure. But we'll discuss that later.

Banks are also too short-sighted. They train staff to focus on policies and programs; don't waive fees, sell the credit card, etc. Do these policies and programs maximize the lifetime value of the customer? Maybe sometimes, but definitely not all the time.

Solving both of those problems requires the integration of a functioning next best action technology. But we'll discuss that later, too.

So, what should a branch do?

The number one rule for branches should be: do only what absolutely, without a doubt requires a human being. That should be a pretty short list. And that short list makes up the limited functionality of the branch of the future.

Yes, it's true that you have little old ladies who like to come into the branch to make their deposits. But don't build the future around a generation that is becoming ever more connected to the Internet.

Those same little old ladies used to bring their passbook savings into the branch to get it stamped, too. You don't still offer those any more, do you?

That list may vary based on the regulations of the geographic area as well as the technology infrastructure of the bank, but think long and hard before putting something on that list. No matter what you decide, be honest with yourself. Too often we design a process to be manual with human interaction in order to artificially engineer a sales conversation with the customer. If you have to engineer it, it's not the right time.

Yes, you may sell some things that way, but if your models were better, smarter, you'd be able to generate that sale in a more efficient and cost-effective way. Besides, when customers come into the branch to buy something, they aren't being "sold." You're just taking an order.

Rules for the Future Branch:
1. Only do in the branch what absolutely, without a doubt requires face-to-face communication.
2. Everything else, do at your own risk. In other words, that transaction is costing more than it should. Do it with your eyes wide open.

THE NEW CONTACT CENTER

In the previous chapter on online versus mobile banking, we discussed a number of technologies available to integrate the online banking application with a live interaction. In this section, I want to focus more on the interaction itself, rather than the technology that facilitates it.

Let's define the contact center. The contact center is a set of employees connected to customers through a number of different interaction technologies (i.e., phone, chat, video, social media, etc.) in order to provide sales, service, and support, whether outbound or inbound. Each of those three functions needs to be focused on a personalized, data-centric experience.

We're going to spend some time on sales in a future chapter, specifically focusing on how to craft a unique and personalized offer to a customer that is relevant and timely. Outbound sales is generally thought of as "cold calling" while inbound sales is generally thought of as "upselling."

I want to dispel both of those notions.

Good outbound or inbound sales is driven via behavioral triggers. Those triggers come from all channels of customer touch points. Transactions and interactions form the source data for sales triggers. By transaction, I mean deposits, withdrawals, payments, or transfers. By interactions, I mean service requests, branch visits, and other day-to-day communication with the bank. Good behavioral models use those data points to create propensity models that help banks prioritize their contacts in a cost-efficient way.

Banks can't chase down every lead without taking into consideration the effectiveness of the sales pitch. Likewise, they can't chase down every lead without an understanding of the potential profitability of the offer they're making.

Whether triggered by transaction or interactions, one thing we know from experience is that sales opportunities grow stale quickly. We need to react to these interactions immediately or they become non-predictive.

One bank in the United States found this out by analyzing the effectiveness of outbound calling triggered by a clickstream analysis of users on the website. When a user, logged in through online banking, researched a particular financial product, the web server inserted a lead into the outbound sales calling queue.

The typical way sales queues are handled is for the oldest lead to be assigned to the next available representative. This queue processing is known as "first-in-first-out." It's the standard by which most sales leads are worked.

The bank learned, however, via experience and through modeling, these leads grew cold quickly. If they didn't react on the lead within a few hours, it was as if the trigger information was useless.

In order to utilize this fact, they changed their queue processing to a "first-in-last-out" model, where the most recent lead was worked by the next available representative. The bank reported a significant increase in conversion rates because the calls were made within the "window of relevancy" for the customer.

Each bank and each sales opportunity is going to have a different window of relevancy. The information gained from this experience, however, is that processing time needs to be a variable in any model built using event-based data. Research shows that sales leads close with higher probability the sooner they're acted upon.

That suggests another important element to any sales infrastructure: real-time data processing.

In both outbound and inbound offer assignment, most banks use a batch process that assigns customers to offers every month or quarter. Such a batch process removes the most relevant data from the decision process—the things that have happened today.

Often we think service is individualized by definition. This is not true. Banks provide service to customers through a combination of information and policy application with the occasional exception thrown in for good measure.

If the bank truly understood the lifetime value of each customer and the impact of service decision on that value, it would be applying a customer-centric service policy instead of managing exceptions. Obviously, consumer fairness laws require some equal treatment across groups. But most government regulation still provides the ability to waive standard policy. The waiver, when applied systematically and prudently, becomes the policy rather than the exception.

It's important then to push these kinds of intelligent decision tools to the front line, so the contact center representatives know as much about the customer as the back-office analytic departments do. And, when they learn the customer situation has changed, as they often do first through contact centers, they can update the decisions based on the new information. Anything else is reactive and suboptimal.

We'll discuss how best to implement these servicing systems in the chapters on Next Best Action.

Finally, we offer support to customers to help them navigate the organization or the financial product they have. Sometimes this is in the form of information, but often support involves context. When the bank has the right context, it can offer the support proactively. I want to focus on that proactive support.

For example, a customer pays a credit card via ACH transfer every month; he first credits a line of credit account and then manually transfers that money onto the credit card. A quick review of the account will indicate that something is wrong. The customer is having difficulty paying the right loan account with the bill payment. The contact center should call the customer proactively with an offer to fix this problem. Such an act demonstrates to the customer that the bank knows his situation and is reacting accordingly.

Recently, satellite TV companies are starting to monitor signal strength to their customers in order to detect installation problems or repair issues before a customer request. This proactive outreach gets to the heart of one of the biggest complaints about satellite TV—bad signal. By addressing the issue head on and proactively, these companies are keeping customer satisfaction and retention high.

Banks can and should apply the same principles. They know when their customers are having trouble. Perhaps they are overdrafting and only make the necessary transfer from savings afterward. Or perhaps they are writing checks of the same amount every month that can easily be replaced by online bill payment. Banks can reach out to these customers directly and offer support to fix these problems.

Unfortunately, many banks still rely on the argument that fixing such customer problems is not profitable—that it would be better to collect the overdraft fees than to sign up a customer for automatic overdraft protection. This argument leads to increased customer distrust and vulnerability to alternative providers who can offer a better service experience. Proceed with this worldview at your own risk.

Rules for the Future Contact Center:
1. Outbound and inbound sales should be based on time-sensitive event triggers and acted upon as quickly as possible.
2. Service policies should take customer lifetime value into consideration, thus changing the exception into the rule.
3. Proactive support is based on data analysis and a realization that customer satisfaction has an impact on lifetime value and thus, revenue.

THE NEW ATM

Two things are critical to remember about the ATM. First, customers are only there to get cash. And second, they're in a hurry. Unless you have something to say about the cash they're trying to get, they have no interest or patience in anything else. It's what I call the ATM rule: don't delay the cash!

So let's drop our crazy ideas about selling credit cards or home equity loans or getting people to opt-in to electronic statements, or even being the vehicle for making transfers or paying bills through the ATM—unless that is explicitly related to the need for cash.

We already know the mobile device will be the central orchestrator of the relationship. That means the ATM of the future will be directed by the mobile device.

In order to improve account security, the ATM of the future will likely incorporate a two-factor authentication process whereby the customer activates it by use of the mobile device, and then has to enter a time-sensitive code provided through the mobile banking application. Or, if the customer needs to use a card, the card's PIN is authenticated with another factor—biometric or time-sensitive token. In fact, this isn't all that futuristic. It's already being implemented in some countries.

Let's review the ATM of today and see how it stacks up against our three basic mistakes of too impersonal, too late, and too short sighted.

Generally, the ATM is fairly personalized and acts in real-time. Where it completely falls short is in being too short sighted.

Remember, the entire purpose of this machine is to get cash. As I pointed out, delaying that function for any other reason is, by definition, short sighted. But more than that, the ATM is a cash-flow tool with no cash-flow management functions. Banks manage part of the cash flow and typically don't let customers take cash out of accounts they don't have.

But what about future cash flow?

Believe it or not, banks sit on all the information they need to project whether a particular cash transaction will lead to cash-flow trouble in the future. They just need to use it.

Imagine a consumer experience where the customer requests cash from the ATM and is met with the following message:

"We noticed that you are requesting $250 from your account. Based on your balance and your transaction history, we think you might overdraft your account next Thursday. Would you like a short-term loan in the amount of $350 to cover that projected shortfall?"

Yes, it interrupts the flow, so you might think it violates my ATM rule: don't delay the cash. But it does so by adding value to the banking relationship, and it even sells a financial product. One that you actually know the customer has a high probability of needing. Sounds like a win-win to me.

There are those bankers who might be thinking: yes, but this erodes our overdraft fee income. I'm going to assume you're not one of those bankers. Banks that think that way are going to lose. They're going to lose to other banks or alternative financial services providers that are growing specifically because they think differently.

There is a big difference between charging someone a fee (or interest) for a service they request and the bank explicitly agreed to provide and then charging someone a fee after the fact—even if they signed up for the protection. Enter into that agreement explicitly. You'll get more money for it anyways.

Of course, there are many more services that can be offered once you start thinking about the ATM as a cash-flow management device. The overdraft avoidance warning is just one of them.

Finally, the big elephant in the cash management room is peer-to-peer (P2P) electronic payments. Much like the discussion about the branch, I wouldn't predict the death of cash, but it is clearly becoming less important. I wouldn't bet against that trend either.

In 2013, 55 million Africans used basic mobile phones to make P2P payments one person to another. Not smart phones. Basic flip phones. If the mobile phone is being used to displace cash, then what is the future for the ATM?

Some futurists predict a cashless economy. In that case, the ATM serves no purpose beyond kiosk banking. The question then becomes, who needs a kiosk?

There are those that try to transform the ATM into something other than a cash-delivery vehicle. I think this is a mistake. The cost associated with deploying and maintaining a network of ATMs is not justified for any other function than cash delivery. If P2P electronic payments take off, prepare for the downgrade of ATMs.

Rules for the Future ATM:
1. Deploy multi-factor authentication centered on the mobile device.
2. Don't delay the cash!
3. The ATM is a cash-flow management device. Leverage it as such.
4. P2P payments will reduce the role of the ATM.

PART III. WHAT SHOULD BANKS DO?

This is the question next best action technology answers, so it's fitting that it is the question that introduces this next section. This, of course, is the second pillar of the bank of the future.

Instead of focusing on the mathematics behind the analytic solution, I want to draw a picture of what life is like with next best action in place.

First we'll analyze the functions of the bank that are most often driven by analytics: marketing, product selection, and pricing. Then we'll turn to the true opportunity: on-boarding, servicing, retention, and collections. Finally, we'll discuss what it takes to get one of these systems up and running.

This section will answer the following questions:

1. What should a customer-centric marketing program look like?
2. How does the bank help a customer select the right set of financial products—at the right price—in a win-win way?
3. In day-to-day interactions with the customer, how do banks know how to react best, engage proactively, and

stop profitable customers from leaving or turning unprofitable?

4. What is involved in getting a next best action system up and running?

CHAPTER 6. NEXT BEST ACTION IN MARKETING, BUNDLING, AND PRICING

I want to start our conversation about the use of analytics in the place that we most often think about customer analytics: marketing, product selection, and pricing.

In each section, I'll assess current efforts against the three big mistakes: too impersonal, too late, and too short sighted. We'll see where the banks are, break down the false narratives that cause them to miss the target, and build back up a strong framework that they can put in place to achieve the bank of the future.

MARKETING

Marketing is about finding the right message for the right customer. In banking, message is about a product offer. There are two components to any product offer: the product itself and the term and conditions of that product.

Since terms and conditions in banking products is really just pricing, we're going to postpone that for a few sections. In the meantime, let's discuss what goes into selecting the right product for the right customer.

Product selection can happen during several opportunities: the initial marketing of a customer and an upsell. Since upsell is just marketing with slightly more available data, we'll treat them similarly.

Let's analyze product selection efforts through the lens of the three big mistakes: too impersonal, too late, and too short sighted.

Banks try to avoid the first by being individual in their product selection recommendations. This may be done through a live sales representative who listens carefully to the needs of the customer and tailors the products to meet their needs. Or, it may occur through automated product selection or offer management technology.

Either way, banks just don't do a very good job. Customers often feel these offers are not relevant or badly timed. Worse yet, the next generation feels very negatively about anything banks have to say. 71% of so-called Millennials would rather go to the dentist than listen to what their bank has to say, and one-third do not even think they will need a bank in the future[10].

The offers are bad because the bank's data is bad. Not wrong, mind you, just bad. And believe it or not, bankers can be very impersonal when we're actually in person.

Don't think so? Ask yourself this: how many bank sales and service representatives offer the same credit card—or whatever the product du jour is—to every customer?

Some banks are making progress here by installing next best offer technology in the branch. They put an individualized offer in front of the branch sales representative. In some cases, they may even wrap it in a personalized script for delivery.

But these systems too often make the second two mistakes; they are too late and too short sighted.

---

[10] "The Millennial Disruption Index". Survey millennialdisruptionindex.com.

They are too late because often these systems are built to analyze customer demographic data that is static. If the customer data banks use to build their next best offer models doesn't change in six months, then the bank must be assuming that over that six-month period the customer has an equal likelihood of buying that product.

That doesn't make any sense.

Customers buy products because events happen in their lives. Those events include moving to a new home, coming into money, losing money or a job, having a child leave the house, or having a new one join the family. There are many others. Some banks can't predict, but for others, they have data, and they're much more predictive of whether a customer buys a financial product than static demographics.

But often banks can *detect*. And that's what's important. Banks don't have to predict an event in the future in order to notice changing customer needs. They just need to detect that event and act on it. Fast!

So, ask yourself, what data is used in your cross-sell models? Is it static? If so, go gather more data and build better models.

Most of the models used today are based on the idea that banks actually *cannot* predict when a customer will buy. They think they may know what the customers want when the time is right. The bank just keeps hounding them until they buy. Not exactly a stellar customer experience.

And there are so many good examples in other industries. Product recommendations from Amazon sometimes feel so "right" that they're a service, not an ad. Although they're still getting the experience dialed in correctly, Google can target ads in ways that are truly scary sometimes.

An example from Google: while browsing a travel website, I saw an ad for something that will keep birds out of my backyard. I thought, how does Google know I have a bird problem in my backyard? (I do. They're awful.) But then I remembered that I had gone to a website weeks ago to buy things to try to keep birds out of my backyard.

Spying on my web traffic? Maybe. If the offer hadn't been relevant, I might have been annoyed to know Google had tracked that history.

But it was relevant and I actually clicked on the ad (something I almost never do). So I was happy they took the time to get to know me enough to start a relevant conversation about a need I actually had.

The analog of Google's web tracking is transaction analysis for banking. In fact, I would argue financial transactions are an even better source of data about what a customer needs and when. Google would argue the same thing, which is why they have invested money in financial services companies. They their hands on the data!

Banks know when the financial transaction pattern of their customers is "different" from the past. It's the basis of every fraud solution in the industry. When the transaction pattern changes, that means our customer's situation has changed. Maybe so much that they need a financial product. Not always, but that's what statistical models are for.

How are product selection efforts short sighted?

Here it comes down to what we're measuring. Most marketing analytics focus on click-throughs or response rates. Models are built to drive volume. But have banks found the most profitable offer for the customer? Something truly beneficial?

The only way to achieve that is to use the right objective in the decision-making. We're not in business solely to drive volume—although sometimes we have short-term volume objectives to cover fixed expenses or to generate market share in certain areas. We're in business to generate profit, long-term profit.

Analytics need to be focused on understanding and maximizing customer lifetime value. It's this metric that drives long-term vision and avoids the short sightedness from which the current analytics often suffer.

This outcome requires the use of optimization—a true next best action framework. It's not enough to rely on traditional A/B testing and response rate maximization. Banks need to understand the drivers of profit and influence their outcome.

Similar to our conclusions about marketing, product selection needs to be smarter and take the long-term actions of the customer into consideration. When that happens, banks have truly found the next best marketing action.

BUNDLING

Bundling is about finding the right combination of products for each individual customer. Of course, like marketing, each product must be priced appropriately. As before, we'll postpone that discussion until the next section.

Right now, let's discuss how to experiment and decide which bundle to offer to each customer and when that offer should be made.

Most banks do not do a lot of active bundling. Perhaps a credit card is cross-sold with a deposit account. A true bundle, however, is something that comes together in one unit. Because this is a fairly new concept, it is difficult to get a data set necessary for statistical modeling. Therefore, most bundling efforts are ad hoc and haphazard.

In theory, banks would test different product bundles on different clients until they found the ones that matched. Given all the products that might be included in a bundle, however, this may not be feasible.

What banks are trying to measure here is called *affinity*. It's the relative value of two products together rather than just one. In retail, they measure affinity all the time even though they have potentially billions of different combinations. They use a technique called market basket analysis.

In banking, they don't have market baskets per se, but they do have customers with multiple products. In order to understand affinity, the banks have to measure sensitivity to offers and price based on those customers who happen to have both products (or all the products in the case of a bundle bigger than two).

Let's look at an example. Let's say you want to bundle a DDA with a credit card. When you go through your customer database, you should segment out those customers who hold both the DDA and the credit card; call them group A. Then you take all customers with the DDA alone; call them group B. Then you take all customers with that credit card alone; call them group C.

Now we need to see if group A customers behave differently than groups B and C. This next paragraph is a brief description of one way you can detect the difference. The analysts may have other ways.

The simplest way to do that is some kind of offer response model or a price sensitivity model on DDA (or credit card) and include groups A and B (or C). Include an indicator for group A membership. If you're assessing pricing sensitivity, you may want to include a price term for just those members of group A. This is called an interaction term.

You know there is some affinity in the bundle if the membership term is statistically significant. (Remember that from your statistics class?) Otherwise, it may be worth bundling together from a marketing perspective, but there's no analytic reason to think of the two as a "bundle."

This technique doesn't measure the strength of the affinity, although the strength of the membership term does provide some information. It is really only there to narrow down the potential bundles you should test. It also doesn't completely eliminate the non-bundles.

For example, you might find that when you explicitly market the DDA with a credit card and explain the great benefits of having them both together, you find affinity where otherwise it doesn't exist. But beyond testing every possible combination, this isn't a bad place to start.

Once you've identified the affinity, it's time to measure it. You have to test the bundle in order to measure affinity. Set aside time to market the bundle and record the data.

In order to create the best test possible, you will want to record every time the bundle was offered, to whom it was offered, what the specifics of the offer were (e.g., price), and what the reaction to the offer was. This way you create a dataset that includes offer response and price sensitivity. You will also want to include a marker for times when customers opt for product 1 or product 2, but not the bundle, as well as the times the customer turns down everything.

When basing pricing decisions, something we'll get to next, you'll want to understand the joint product profitability. In the case of a deposit-loan bundle, it will be the sum of the earnings credit and interest revenue (however you choose to define it) from the two products. If you gain some kind of cost savings from the bundling (e.g., lower origination expenses or servicing expenses), then make sure to indicate such. That will make the bundle even more attractive and allow you to price it appropriately.

Now the bundle is just another financial product in the portfolio. It can be analyzed and treated like single products. But one thing that is unique about product bundling is the measurement of price sensitivity.

In the case of product bundles that contain two prices, such as a deposit-loan combination or even a loan-loan combination, the statistical model to measure acceptance based on price has two price variables in it—one for each product. When the bank makes optimal pricing decisions, it'll actually be deciding on two variables separately (although not independently).

The value in this analysis is that it separates customer sensitivity into two pieces—one for each product. This separation is what banks try to estimate when they have loss leader pricing.

You may find that the customer is much more sensitive to the credit card rate than the DDA interest rate. The joint profitability, however, may be such that you can lower the credit card rate slightly, keep longevity in the DDA, which increases the earnings credit and actually increases the joint profit of both products. This is a balancing act that is difficult to do without sufficient analytics and profitability analysis behind it.

Loss leader pricing without this kind of bundled product analysis is like walking a tightrope without a net.

Get a net.

By understanding the value proposition of product bundles, it adds to our list of next best product actions. Banks can include sophisticated offers and understand how they maximize the customer's lifetime value while meeting internal goals.

PRICING

You can make an argument that pricing is the most important function that exists within the bank. I wouldn't disagree.

In fact, not only is pricing one of the top motivators when customers choose a bank, it's the most efficient way to increase profitability.[11]

The challenge with pricing is that it affects everything about the bank's portfolio, but often so little of that information is used to inform the decision. Pricing will affect profitability; that is obvious. But it also affects default rates, prepayment, the mix of customers, the volume the bank generates, and our brand proposition. Ignoring these factors leads to the bank's detriment.

---

[11] "Sizing the Price: The Power of Pricing", Deloitte, Journal of Professional Pricing, 2012.

Banking pricing comes in two basic flavors: individual pricing and rate sheet pricing. Individual pricing provides the flexibility to set the price at the individual level, based on their individual characteristics. With rate sheet pricing, the bank groups like customers into segments, whether well-defined like boxes on a rate sheet or something more complex like a decision tree. They have some kind of rule or map that tells them how to map a customer into a box, and they get that price.

In theory, individual pricing is always preferable to rate sheet pricing. The ability to adjust pricing for each individual customer gives the bank maximum flexibility to hit the goals it has and to create the exact portfolio mix they're looking for.

In practice, however, individual pricing may be difficult or impossible to do. There are three major reasons individual pricing may be complex: regulatory, IT infrastructure, and market acceptance.

Regulatory barriers are obvious. In some countries, it is prohibited to differentiate price beyond some well-established dimensions. Geographic differentiation may be forbidden, as it is in some European countries. In addition, some countries require banks to justify their pricing dimensions by connecting them to cost in order to demonstrate a "true financial need" for differentiation.

These regulatory hurdles rarely serve the public good the way they are intended. But this chapter isn't about the pros and cons of government regulation. The rules are what they are, and whatever they are, banks need to follow them.

More annoying, however, are IT infrastructure limitations. These are restrictions for which there are no excuses. They are problems of the bank's own making.

Often times, pricing execution systems are only able to store a limited number of price variables or sometimes even a limited number of prices. In those cases, banks are limited to the number of segments we can create. Not only is individual pricing impossible, but a deep level of segmentation and robust rate sheet development may also be impeded.

You can run a cost-benefit analysis to fixing this problem. Using pricing optimization systems, you can approximate the lift that would come from the marketplace by creating additional tradeoffs through individual (or even robust rate sheet) pricing. Comparing that benefit to estimated IT costs for fixing the system will provide the business case (or not) for making the appropriate changes.

Very often, this effort is well worth the cost, but a bank's mileage may vary.

Finally, there may be issues around market acceptance for individualized pricing. Generally speaking, customers are not open to individualized pricing unless there is good reason. The reason individual pricing of loans is more common than of deposits is because of the practice of risk-based pricing.

Customers apply for loans, and then based on their credit score, a price is quoted. This price will often include an adjustment for individual risk, but can also include increased margin for that risk or other margin adjustments based on the individual's willingness to pay. This leverage of price sensitivity is increasingly common in consumer loan pricing.

Deposit pricing, on the other hand, is less likely to include individual pricing except in cultures where negotiated bank pricing is accepted practice or where the customer value is high enough to justify exception-pricing processes. Fundamentally, however, this comes down to the question of transparency. When customers are accustomed to transparent pricing before applying, they will not tolerate individual pricing. Where the practice is pricing is based on application data, individual pricing is often an option.

Let me provide one last note on individual pricing. Often times the question is asked: how do you do individual pricing when a new customer walks through the door you don't know anything about? The answer is on creating some rule that allows a bank to "match" the new, unknown customer to one that it does know.

That can be done in a number of different ways. First, it may segment existing customers into groups by characteristics known at the time the new customer applies, choose some kind of "average" price for that group, and look up that "average" price for the new customer.

Sounds like rate-sheet pricing, right? Yes, it does. There are two other more sophisticated approaches, which feel similar, but have no concept of rate sheets.

The first alternative is to create a reverse-engineered formula for individual pricing. Whether as mathematical formula or decision tree, the bank can develop a mathematical map that takes the individual characteristics of existing customer to predict their individual prices. Then when a new customer walks through the door, it applies that mathematical map.

The only difference between rate sheet pricing and reverse engineered pricing is that it's usually not an easy lookup table. The biggest challenge, therefore, is implementation in a price execution system. Pricing systems are good at handling tree-based pricing schemes; so often, this is the preferred route. But the bank could choose a mathematical formula as well, but the implementation challenges can often be formidable.

The second alternative is the use of "nearest neighbor" techniques. This technique is a type of clustering algorithm that allows you to find an existing customer that "looks like" the new one. The bank then gives that existing customer's price.

That's all I'll say about nearest neighbor techniques. This isn't a book on data mining, but you can read more about such techniques in books like that.

So, what about the core proposition of this book: creating a personalized banking experience? Can that be done without individualized pricing?

The answer is yes. Even with formula-based or rate sheet pricing, each customer can be catered to individually. The trick is finding the right level of segmentation and pricing. Obviously, as stated before, this needs to be balanced against pricing regulations you are subject to, but almost every bank I've been in has room to make pricing more granular. You may not get pricing to a segment of one, but closer is better.

Whether a bank decides to leverage price sensitivity or not, measuring it is no longer an option. Price sensitivity is the way to assess how prices will be received in the marketplace. It is the basic reaction that the bank tries to guess when it sets prices.

If you've ever been in a pricing committee meeting where someone says, "we know that a 10 basis point decrease in prices generally results in a 3% increase in volume," you've just heard a price-sensitivity heuristic.

The challenge, however, is two-fold: heuristics are not granular enough to measure the differences between types of customers and they're not specific enough to be useful. But every bank has a heuristic, and heuristics don't create personalized banking experiences.

We'll discuss the implementation of pricing systems in a future chapter, but it's important to know how leveraging price sensitivity changes the dynamic of the pricing process.

Consider the typical pricing process today. A pricing committee meets every few weeks, let's say. It generally consists of stakeholders from different parts of the bank with very different goals. Marketing and sales are usually focused on volume. Risk and finance are generally focused on profit. Compliance is generally focused on keeping the CEO out of jail. And in the middle of it all is usually product management, whose goals often change with the business.

Because most banks do not have a central data repository that captures the impact of price changes on volumes, each member comes to the meeting with their own data and view of what just happened since the last meeting. I call this the "battle of the spreadsheets."

Sales and marketing come with origination numbers and competitive prices in tow. Risk and finance have profitability and default numbers. Compliance comes with the latest regulatory guidance. And product management comes with marching orders from the CEO in tow. "Grow volume by 5%. Increase margins by 3%. Go!"

No one knows exactly what to do.

Most pricing processes devolve into a comparison with competitive pricing, figuring others know generally how to price and besides, you can't be too far off the competition anyways. The group argues a little, throws a dart at a dartboard, stays comfortably within the competitive margins, and makes parallel shifts in price across all segments.

As far as industries go, banking is one of the least sophisticated in our pricing processes. But with alterative players on the edges of our industry making a run at our customers, we cannot stay this way and survive.

Up until now, the mantra has been, "you get what you misprice." This attitude has created a very risk-adverse atmosphere when it comes to using more sophisticated pricing techniques.

But in the not too distant future the mantra will be, "price it right or die." And the death of our business from competitors who can manage data better than we can does tend to focus the mind. In a future chapter, we'll talk about how to put a personalized pricing system in place, whether that system outputs individual pricing or segmented pricing. That pricing sophistication is a key component to finding the next best price—if you will—that enhances or product offers and maximizes the long-term value of customers.

Next Best Offer Recap:
Whether marketing a new product, generating bundles, or finding the right price for those products, we've just discussed what is often referred to as "Next Best Offer."

To paraphrase a very interesting man, I don't always have something to sell, but when I do, it should be the best thing possible.

To summarize, there are three major pieces of any offer:

1. The core product offering
2. Other products that can be bundled
3. The price offered

All three of these things need to be personalized for each individual customer and prospect. This path to personalization starts by building three key models:

1. Response
2. Affinity
3. Sensitivity

Those three metrics are not the end all be all of the decision. Clearly, banks are out to make a profit, gain volume, manage risk, etc. A next best offer decision system needs to take those three metrics as inputs to the process and leverage them to generate the right offer, bundle, and price to each customer that meets those objectives.

But what if they're not selling anything? Or shouldn't be selling anything? The same basic methods can be used to understand what to do in between the buying moments.

CHAPTER 7. NEXT BEST ACTION IN SERVICING, RETENTION, AND COLLECTIONS

In between the selling moments, there are still valuable interactions banks have with their customers. They often think of them all as "servicing," but they can actually break them down into four different categories: on-boarding, servicing, retention, and collections.

Day-to-day interactions can be grouped together as part of the customer service experience. These may involve providing information or support to the existing relationship. Banks often neglect this part of the job, but customers claim how their relationship is serviced matters a great deal.

There are two specific servicing tasks, which I want to address separately: retention and collection. Retention is where some action is taken to react to the risk of a customer closing their account and leaving the bank. Collection, a type of retention, is mitigating the loss of revenue associated with a default, whether from a loan or an unpaid over-drafted deposit account.

In both of these cases, the bank can choose to be proactive or reactive. Most banks choose the reactive path, preferring to wait until they have more information before they act hastily in a way that may degrade their portfolio value.

This may be the right choice, but it is rarely the right choice for every customer. Creating a personalized banking experience depends on crafting a retention and collection plan that takes the individual characteristics—and long-term profitability—of the customer into consideration when deciding how to act or what policy should be.

We'll discuss each in detail.

SERVICING

Servicing should be considered as any interaction that occurs between account opening and account closing. As mentioned, we'll handle retention and collection conversations separately. But the very first interaction after the customer decides to buy is a set of tasks we call "on-boarding."

Research tells us that on-boarding is a key moment—that acquisition moment—where the bank affects the long-term trajectory of the customer. In a recent survey of banks, nine out of ten indicated that they believe the onboarding process impacts customer lifetime value.[12] Handling these tasks correctly can increase the overall profitability of the customer.

There could be a whole book just on creating a better on-boarding process for banking customers. Frankly, the industry needs it. Banks could make a great deal of progress by focusing on paper reduction, process redesign, and customer satisfaction. But that's not the purpose of this section.

Since the on-boarding process is so central to setting the tone of the future relationship, there are several things that can be done here to personalize the experience. It's well known that on-boarding is a very good time to sell additional related products.

---

[12] "Client-Centric Onboarding – Hopes and Realities for Global Banks", Forrester Consulting on behalf of Pegasystems, May 2014.

Therefore, any on-boarding experience should include a next best offer query in order to see if a bundle or other separate product is a relevant and profitable offer.

One thing that will completely undermine the upsell at on-boarding is the efficiency of the bank's process. If it takes 30 minutes to open a deposit account, you can bet the customer will not sit through another on-boarding process to add on that credit card. So before spending too much time integrating cross-sell into the on-boarding process, make sure what the bank has today is tolerable.

From on-boarding through some retention or collection conversation are a series of interactions that will either delight or discourage the customer. We have already talked about how to use the mobile experience as a central conductor of the banking relationship. So here I want to focus less on the "what" and more on the "why."

The purpose of the banking relationship is to create long-term, satisfied customers which generate bottom-line revenue for shareholders or—in the case of a credit union—members. So how do we measure our relative success in creating that value through our daily servicing interactions?

One way that banks historically have measured the success of their servicing efforts is through customer satisfaction. In fact, some banks have confused themselves by thinking the end goal of servicing is to maximize customer satisfaction. This is wrong. It may be that the cost of very high customer satisfaction in certain areas is offset by the overall benefit.

There is only one way to determine the appropriate levels of customer satisfaction. Quantifying the benefit is the key. By asking and monitoring customer satisfaction scores, banks are able to connect the dots between particular interactions and profitability.

That statement may seem bold since most banks could not tell you the value of customer satisfaction as a monetary measure today. But if banks are collecting satisfaction data at the customer level and connecting that to a lifetime value calculation, then they have the tools to build a business case for customer satisfaction.

For example, one major US-based credit card issuer was able to quantify the increased net present value of the customer by moving up one additional point on their customer service scale. It was not linear; moving from a 1 to a 2 was different than moving from a 4 to a 5. But they were able to quantify the value of customer satisfaction. And from that quantification, they were able to develop business cases to support investment in training, systems, and customer satisfaction programs.

Many practitioners across verticals rely on the net-promoter score (NPS) to assess the satisfaction level of their customers. While I don't have a problem with NPS per se, I do not like relying on made-up metrics for decision-making. Instead, metrics are inputs into optimal decision processes, which maximize revenue.

If you've done the work to quantify customer satisfaction to increase in customer value, it doesn't really matter which metric you use, as long as you can tie them together in a way that predicts profit changes by what you do.

In order to support quantification of customer satisfaction, survey programs need to follow a few guidelines:

1. Do not measure customer satisfaction anonymously.

2. Measure customer satisfaction after key interactions and code that score to the interaction (as well as the employee or employees involved).
3. Even if you do not have a reliable lifetime profitability metric, monitor changes in satisfaction at the customer level and correlate them to major account activity, such as withdrawals, account openings, or other service requests.

So, how does the measurement and quantification of customer satisfaction create a personalized banking experience?

RETENTION

Retaining customers is often cited as one of the major strategic goals of banks around the world. The challenge most banks face is in understanding how to retain customers profitably.

In fact, customer retention is a four-part problem.

1. Is there a coming retention issue?
2. Is the customer worth retaining?
3. What program should I offer to retain the customer?
4. What terms and conditions of that program should I offer?

Each of these decisions comes in sequence and with its own sets of problems for measuring and deciding. And the core objective, long-term customer profitability, is a function of all four parts.

Many banks don't even ask the first question: is there a coming retention issue? Being proactive about retention has several benefits. Research shows us that offering a retention program before a customer indicates his intention to leave is more likely to be successful and requires less monetary value to achieve that success, compared to efforts made after a customer decides to leave.

So although many banks don't like to "give away the farm" to customers unless they have to, with the appropriate predictive models and decisioning[13] systems, they can often save money on their retention programs if they engage proactively.

Models that predict customer attrition successfully are event based. In fact, similar to models built to predict fraud, attrition-prediction models are built on understanding how a series of events in turn builds up to cause a customer to leave. Analytic techniques such as Complex Event Processing (CEP) are often helpful to detect not just the events to watch for, but the order and timing of those events.

For example, consider the following series of events. A customer calls the contact center to ask for a fee waiver. Then the customer visits the branch and complains. Then the customer tweets that his "bank ripped me off." Then the customer moves a large sum of money out of an account.

Each one of these events separately may not be a concern, but taken together, they represent a serious problem. On top of that, these events may occur over several days and the bank may not have the analytic horsepower today to react.

Other verticals are making huge strides in applying complex event processing to predict customer behavior. Hürriyet, one of the largest newspapers in Turkey, uses CEP to find behaviors of web visitors which predict interest and churn.[14]

---

[13] Decisioning is a term now commonly used to refer to a class of technologies that help enterprises make better decisions.

[14] "Application Story: Real Time Churn Prediction and Offering", Julian Clark, Complex Events, March 2014.

Assuming a bank can predict that it has a retention issue, or perhaps a customer has announced his intention to leave, the bank must now ask if the customer is worth retaining?

Traditionally this question has been answered through some sort of customer segmentation. The service representative would look at a screen to see if the customer was premier or in collections, etc. The problem with this approach is that it assumes retention value can be assessed without understanding the cost to retain.

Since there may be several programs available to the representative, each program will have a separate cost associated with it. It is impossible to know whether you should act without knowing what that action should be.

Thus, the final two questions—what and how much— become critical to understanding the appropriate action. Your bank has defined a set of retention programs it may offer. In addition, each program may contain a sliding scale value associated with it.

For example, if a bank is trying to prevent a loan customer from refinancing, it may offer a refinance of its own. That refinance package comes with an interest rate (and other terms). The bank cannot decide the cost of the refinance package without understanding the suggested term and conditions.

What this dual approach does is split up the decision into a discrete choice of program and a continuous choice of price. And once the bank can calculate the cost of each program along with the value potentially lost if it is not successful, it now has an optimal retention strategy.

So let's pull these all together.

1. Complex event processing provides a probability of attrition given a series of timed events.
2. A set of relevant retention programs is selected for each customer based on his portfolio, segment, and other eligibility criteria.
3. A response model calculates the probability of success when a retention program is offered to a particular customer. There is a different response model for each program, which includes variables that quantify the terms of the program.
4. The cost of each program—along with the chosen terms— is calculated and compared against the cost of doing nothing.
5. The cost of doing nothing is defined as the loss of all revenue if the customer has announced his intention to leave, or the expected loss of revenue if the bank is predicting attrition through a CEP model.
6. Choose the option with the lowest cost (or highest future revenue).

Clearly, running such a program requires live systems and real-time calculation capabilities. If the bank integrates CEP event detection, alerting systems will also need to be included. But the end result is a retention-decision system built to react individually and personally to each customer's set of circumstances.

So when an annoyed customer is reached out to proactively to fix his problem, instead of negatively tweeting about his bank, he will instead feel that his banking experience is uniquely and satisfyingly personal. And that is the goal.

COLLECTIONS

Until the credit crisis hit full on in 2009, collections operations were considered a back-office function that didn't really benefit from customer analytics. Fast forward several years and things have changed dramatically.

Gone are the days when a bank of collectors banged away at the phones trying to make right-party contacts and threatening to get the bum borrower to pay up. Banks without a strategy for collections now trail behind those that do—along with hedge funds that specialize in generating cash flow from non-performing assets. Add to that the projection of lost revenue over the next ten years of customers who were treated badly during the most recent downturn and additional cost due to increased regulation, and you have a problem that desperately needs analytics to solve it.[15]

Looking at the possible collections strategies, there is a two-dimensional matrix. (See Figure 3.) Along one dimension, we have proactive and reactive strategies. Across the other, we have several major categories of treatments. Broadly, we'll consider no contact, one-time settlement, modification, no negotiation, and outsource.

Since by proactive, we mean reaching out to a customer before he has hit a certain default target, outsourcing along the proactive dimension doesn't make sense.

Because of the complexity of the different strategies, there are a series of behavioral models that are needed to analyze their impact. Fortunately, there is overlap between the collections strategies whether executed proactively or reactively, so we can establish the framework for each regardless of how it's executed.

---

[15] "As regulators target debt collectors, attorneys warn banks to rethink selling defaulted credit card debt," Joe Taylor, CardRating.com, August 2013.

	Proactive	Reactive
No Action	✓	✓
One-time Settlement	✓	✓
Modification	✓	✓
No Negotiation	✓	✓
Outsource (or Sale)	✗	✓

Figure 3. Collection Treatment Matrix

Before we dig into these individual strategies, let's outline some broad guidance for borrower behavior post-default. Historically, collections models underperform risk models in their predictive power. The reason for this difference in model fit is that behavior post-default tends to be very individualized to the unique economic situation of the borrower. These items are usually opaque to the bank; there is no data to collect for analysis. The bank does know that the drivers of loan behavior change dramatically at key points in the default cycle. So it is important that specific collections models be built reflecting these changes.

The key behavioral turning points in loan behavior are the following:

- Repeated delayed payment from historical trend
- Formal late payment
- 30 days delinquency
- 90 days delinquency
- 180 days delinquency

To clarify the first point, many banks have noted that when customers start paying their bill later in the cycle than they have in the past, it's an indication of financial stress. If banks are not tracking this metric, they need to start. It's an easy way to start identifying potential problems before they begin.

What does it mean that drivers of behavior change as delinquency increases? Traditional credit scoring techniques, such as FICO, are very good for measuring the default probably of otherwise good borrowers. Once a borrower goes into delinquency, all bets are off. For example, one financial services data firm found that once a mortgage was 30 days past due, FICO explained only 7% of the variation in payment behavior. For an industry that has based its repayment models on credit scoring, such a low explanatory power is a bit of a shock.

But if we think about it, it shouldn't be that surprising. Delinquency represents a combination of financial distress and customer behavior much different from credit scoring. I like to think about these dimensions broadly as CHIA:

- Capacity
- Hardship
- Intent
- Asset

Capacity represents the borrower's ability to handle the debt. You can think of this broadly as income, but it's more than that. It's really disposable income that is available to service the debt. Typically this information is not available unless specifically requested of the borrower.

Often banks verify income as part of the application process, but by the time the loan is delinquent or even in danger of becoming delinquent, income and expenses have usually changed dramatically. As part of the collections efforts, banks often re-verify this information with its borrowers in order to assess the situation anew.

Hardship is a temporary situation in which a borrower cannot make good on his obligations. This situation may be due to medical problems, unemployment, changes in family status, or other unforeseen problems. Because hardship is not a measurable variable, this typically needs to be spotted in regular credit reports. If centralized credit bureaus are not available, this will be a difficult dimension to predict.

The metric to watch for with hardship is to see degrading performance on other credit lines. Historically, mortgage portfolio managers used this metric because the conventional wisdom was that the mortgage would be the last tradeline to see a delinquency. Most recent credit crisis completely invalidated that assumption.

Now some customers tend to protect liquidity first, which means credit cards may be the last to go delinquent. This change underscores the importance of good borrower segmentation.

Intent is the boogeyman of credit risk. It represents the moral component of making good on loan payments. The strength of the intent dimension will vary by geography as it is driven almost exclusively by the downstream consequences of default.

For countries with strict bankruptcy guidelines and strong negative credit reporting bureaus, intent may be less of an issue since the consequences of default are high. On the flip side, geographies with no strong central credit reporting facilities or weak bankruptcy guidelines may find this dimension more potent. Again, customer segmentation is key.

With the dimension asset, I do not mean the total assets of the borrower. The concept of borrower assets belongs to the dimension capacity. Here, I mean the status of the asset upon which the loan is based. And thereby, I'm only referring to secured loans.

One thing the industry learned the hard way during the mortgage crisis of 2008–2009 is that the equity in the home was the number one driver of borrower behavior post-default. In fact, one data analytics company reported that if you ran a search over all relevant borrower metrics, the most predictive metric was the cumulative loan-to-value ratio (CLTV) of the home. More stunning than that, was that the breakpoint (without any coaching from the analysts) was 102%.

The learning there was that borrowers with assets underwater performed one way while borrowers with assets "in the money" performed another. Looking back, this is not a surprise; prior to the crisis, however, almost no bank or collection company was using equity position as a major factor in collections decisions. Today that is no longer the case.

As we analyze different models and variables, we'll keep our CHIA model in mind.

Proactive vs. Reactive Collections

Let's first discuss the difference between proactive and reactive collections strategies. Broadly defined, a proactive collection strategy involves reaching out to a customer before he hits a particular default target. That may mean before he misses his first payment or it may mean before he moves from one delinquency bucket to another.

Many banks are reluctant to engage a customer proactively on collections matters. First, they feel like the conversations are typically strained and uncomfortable, so why go out of your way to engage in them? But more importantly, if the bank engages too early with a customer who eventually does not default, you may be giving away value in a loan relationship that is unnecessary. But this concern comes down to predictive capabilities.

Reactive collections strategies are, of course, more common. Once a particular trip wire has been crossed, the collections department jumps into gear. Many banks have split their departments into teams organized by the time of delinquency. They have names such as "pre-collections" and "loss mitigation."

It may be the right thing to do to split up teams this way, but that decision should be based on analysis that shows all customers in these buckets should be treated similarly. You may find, after such an analysis, that collections teams should be organized by customer segment, rather than by time of delinquency. And by customer segment, I'm referring to a collections segment, not a marketing segment. As I mentioned, once default hits, all bets are off. That customer is going to be very different, and a new segmentation assignment should occur.

Classification of Collection Strategies

Let's move onto the different classifications of collection treatment. There are x different strategies:

1. No contact
2. One-time settlement
3. Modification
4. No negotiation
5. Outsource

The obvious ones is no contact. Collection managers will tell you that most collection efforts are fruitless. Either the customer has no capacity to make good on the debt or has no intention of doing so. In cases where the models can predict that the cost of collection exceeds the expected value in the collection effort, stop trying to collect.

The one-time settlement offer is a common option for smaller consumer loans. These settlements have also become popular for subordinate lien loans where the property is underwater and the likelihood of collecting anything through foreclosure is small. In order to evaluate whether this strategy is the best, banks need to assess the value of the offer versus the expected value of all the other attempted collection measures.

Assuming the borrower has some capacity (and, of course, the intent to do something), the one-time settlement is a good fallback position for borrowers with significant hardship. As we'll see with modification, all other payment options require forecasting cash flow into the future. When the future is murky, or downright bad, settlement is the best option.

Loan modification has come into its own over the last seven years. The mortgage crisis in the US forced banks and investment firms to modify payments on millions of mortgages. These modifications were generally considered unsuccessful, but unsuccessful is a relative term. They were unsuccessful compared to what? To collecting on the mortgages through foreclosure and traditional hard-ball tactics? I'm not so sure that these modifications were all that bad of an option when compared with other alternatives. But history will be the judge.

There are several analytic challenges in assessing the applicability of a modification. First, the key metric here is the net present value of future cash flow. Depending on how delinquent the loan is, one may assume the current value of the asset is zero (or the net of property value and legal costs associated with its repossession and resale). Therefore, what the bank wants to do is maximize the expected cash flow.

Understanding expected cash flow of distressed assets brings us to another class of analytic models called survival models. Borrowed from the insurance arena, survival models predict the likelihood of an object's survival at a time in the future. Much like the actuarial tables of the insurance industry, banks can measure the survivability of future payments in a modification.

Note that this technique is very different from default analysis techniques used for performing loan portfolios. While default probabilities are usually defined over a 12-month period for performing loans, modified loans may not survive 12 months, and therefore, understanding the likelihood of getting a few payments before re-default is critical. Traditional methods of calculating logistic probabilities of default do not suffice and end up undervaluing the cash flow of a modification.

The challenge here is that most banks do not have analysts with sufficient experience in survival modeling. The analytic techniques are very different than standard regression analysis. They involve complex topics, such as censoring and time-varying covariates. My advice is to get professional help.

The treatment of no negotiation is the most popular. It leaves the value of the distressed asset in the hands of collections agents trying to talk the borrower into making his payment and lawyers who will threaten and perhaps eventually bring legal proceedings against the borrower. Analysis of this treatment method includes a good understanding of the geographic impacts of different legal venues and the costs of pursuing such a path.

For secured assets, this treatment may make some sense, even if only as a backup strategy. If the bank has a good handle on its legal costs and a sense of time to monetization, it can know the worst-case scenario by netting the asset value by the legal costs, discounted by time to collection. If none of your other options are better than this, the legal option may be best.

For unsecured loans, the legal option is murkier. Often banks will utilize the legal option not to collect from a borrower, but instead to punish them. The long-term value of such strategies is unknown. But what is known is that other organizations have done some amazing things with non-performing assets by treating the borrowers with some respect. Again, the character (i.e., intent) of the borrower is critical, thus segmentation may be required.

Finally, banks have the chance to send account to outside vendors for collection. Typically, this is done with a negotiated percentage—the remainder going to the vendor who can generate the cash flow—or a full sale of the asset based on a percentage of the face value. Depending on the cost to transfer these loans, and depending on vendors accepting "leftovers" at a reasonable price, outsourcing collections may be preferable to the "do nothing" strategy.

Sometimes outside collection vendors have special skills in skip tracing or other techniques necessary to track down borrowers who chronically cannot be contacted. Maybe they even have better analytics than you and can tease out value where you couldn't find it.

Considering all the possible treatment strategies, next best action technology calculates the long-term value of each strategy and finds the best for each borrower. In this sense, it's similar to marketing optimization, next best offer, because a discrete choice of collection strategy must be made.

But to make it more complex, several treatments have a complex pricing component as well. Settlements must be chosen with a bottom line value. Modifications must come with new terms and conditions, whether interest rate, new term of the loan, or a re-amortization. And finally, sale or outsourcing of the asset may also come with a percentage or commission value.

In each of these cases, next best action must find the right strategy and terms to maximize the lifetime value of the asset—if not the customer as a whole.

Next Best Action Recap:
Once the product has been sold, the hard work really starts. Everything that happens between the time the account is opened and the time the customer closes the account is called "servicing."

There are, however, two very specific kinds of servicing that need to be addressed separately. Those moments are retention and collection.

Let's start at the beginning. The most critical moment in the life of a new customer is the on-boarding experience. Research shows that banks have a great opportunity to set the relationship off on the right track by providing value-added offers. Those offers will not be accepted at the rate they should, however, if the bank cannot do an efficient job opening the new account.

Recall the major questions a bank needs to be able to answer to effectively perform a personalized and profitable retention campaign:

1. Is the customer in danger of attrition?

2. Is the customer worth keeping?
3. What program should I offer the customer?
4. What terms and conditions of that program should I offer the customer?

Finally, should the bank have to engage in a collections conversation with its customer, there are two modes:

- Proactive, where the banks reaches out to the customer before an issue has occurred
- Reactive, where the banks waits until a particular delinquency event has occurred

There are also five basic treatment types:

- No contact
- One-time settlement
- Modification
- No negotiation
- Outsource (sell)

Each of these treatment types has a different analytic problem associated with them. Once a bank is able to assign a future value to each of the treatment types for a customer, it can choose the treatment with the highest value.

Of course, if it has a portfolio of distressed assets it's managing together, the bank may have overall goals around cash flow timing or monies collected that it has to hit. In that case, the decisioning problem is a little more complex, but starts with the same basic analytic structure.

CHAPTER 8. THE FOUNDATION OF NEXT BEST ACTION: DATA, METRICS, AND MODELS

We've spent a great deal of time outlining what a next best action–oriented bank looks like and how they interact with customers. Let's now turn our attention to what it takes to get a next best action decision system up and running.

We in the industry have made the mistake in the past of taking the technology of next best action and splitting it up into component parts: marketing analytics, pricing optimization, proactive retention, etc. That is an error.

The true power of next best action is that it spans the lifecycle of the customer. That same system that recommends a product today will suggest a service recovery tomorrow. If banks design systems that partition knowledge into point solutions, they'll never achieve the benefits they're looking for.

They need them all in one place.

Like any analytic framework, next best action requires four major steps: data, metrics, models, and decisions. I'll start out with the first three that form the foundation for the decisions we make.

The concept of data requires little definition, but it's important to remember that data does not equal information. We'll discuss those data elements that form the source of a next best action framework.

Metrics are just derived data elements. When the bank takes source data and turns them into a new piece of information, it creates a metric. The traditional definition of metric also includes the concept of measurement. Metrics are typically the basis for evaluating a system for success. That connotation applies here as well.

The word model is dangerous. There are probably as many definitions of model as there are people. But in this case, I define model as a statistical process that predicts a certain outcome. For example, a mathematical formula that takes in data about the customer, data about the bank, and returns the probability that the customer behaves in a certain way is a statistical model. And it is those types of models I want to focus on.

DATA

Data sources to understand customer behavior fall into three major categories: customer data, bank data, and external data. Each of those categories breaks down into different types. Not all data is relevant for every type of customer interaction I've described, but many are.

There is no single data dictionary that will be useful for all banks. Some data is necessary, and I'll point out what a bank needs to have. Some data is helpful but optional. In those cases, it will be a matter of deciding if you have it or where you can get it.

Customer Data

There are four major sources of customer data, some of which you have and some of which you may not be collecting today. Each data source is linked together by some customer identifier. The list of sources should serve as a guide for future work, not a "must have" checklist where you reject the ability to use next best action technology if you can't check each box.

The first major category of customer data is *account opening/origination data*. This data set typically is in the account opening or loan origination system. It involves an account-by-account list of all applications, the customers or prospects who submitted the application and the state of the application whether accepted, rejected, or pending.

In some jurisdictions, banks are required to purge personal information from their systems on prospects who did not become customers after a certain time period. This requirement is regarding the personally identifiable information. Your bank should, however, keep the relevant application information, which is not personally identifiable if possible. Rejected application data provides a window into the potential customers the bank does not have, whether it be because of bank or customer rejection. It is a wealth of information; do not discard it. Simply strip off the personally identifiable information and keep the rest.

Customer analytics datamarts typically include an extract as a key source of information. It will include (where applicable) such things as:

- Application date
- Closing date
- Product type and terms
- Price quoted, offered, and booked
- Customer information at the time of application
- Application underwriting status
- Application final disposition

These are broad themes and are not meant to be a field-level view of the data set. But, when they apply to the situation, they are often helpful in understanding the status of the product and customer at the time they applied to open an account.

The next major category of customer data is *customer relationship management data*. As aptly named, this data often sits inside the bank's customer relationship management (CRM) system. It contains a current view of the customer, though often it may also contain a historical list of major changes.

In some banks, the CRM data is not centralized. In that case, the CRM data is used from the relevant line of business depending on the decision to be made, or the CRM, data is brought together from various sources to be merged.

Merging data sources can be challenging because the same data element may exist in multiple systems. That data element may not be the same between systems; in fact, though similarly named, it may not even mean the same thing.

There are two major ways of handling this kind of merging problem. Often, the bank undertakes a data reconciliation project, where differences are tracked and fixed based on the size of the problem and relevance to the business. The bank may choose, however, to leave different versions of the same data element in the final extract rather than reconciling them and letting the modeling and decision-making phase sort out which version(s) are useful. There are many fuzzy techniques to analyze this kind of data, which we'll touch on toward the end of the book.

CRM datasets typically include information about the history of the customer's relationship. Typical metrics may include such things as:

- Number of months as a customer
- Number of accounts the customer has
- Balance of deposits for the customer
- Total outstanding loans for the customer
- Customer segment
- Geographic information
- Customer demographics (in some jurisdictions)
- Current status of customer (in collections, active, inactive, etc.)
- Date of last offer
- Last offer made

The third category of customer data is *transaction data*. Transaction data comes directly from the core system or the loan servicing system. It contains every debit and credit for the product in question.

Typically, transaction data is rarely used for customer analytics, although its use in fraud and anti-money laundering (AML) applications is well known. One reason for its oversight is its sheer volume.

To use transaction data, banks need to rely on big data techniques. Though transaction data is not unstructured, its volume and velocity qualify it for big data treatment. Parallel processing is required to handle data at this volume for most real-time decision-making solutions.

Without resorting to such big data tactics, however, many banks are able to generate great value from the transaction data by using summary metrics. It's common to take large volumes of data and summarize things to make them storable. For example, you might calculate the number of days since the last debit card transaction. Or you might calculate the average daily balance for a customer. These summary statistics are easier to use and several relevant ones may already exist in your CRM database.

The fourth and final category of customer data is *interaction data*. This data set is most often not stored by banks. It is, however, the most worthwhile in terms of being able to make a consistently relevant offer, to react to service issues as they occur, and to make the customer feel like the entire banking experience is built around them.

For many banks, this isn't even a matter of storage; it's a matter of collection. If you think about all the places a bank interacts with the customers—across all channels—it likely does not have any system where they could record what happened.

The electronic channels are the easy ones. Some banks are starting to record major clickstream activity and store it in the customer file. It wouldn't be difficult to record ATM activity and do likewise. Notes can be stored at the contact center when a customer calls. The teller at the branch has similar functionality available, but how many actually do that?

Every interaction carries some information with it. It's just a matter of storing it and then using it to understand the customer better.

Here are several things to consider while developing an interaction data framework:

1. Come up with a list of what you think may be relevant interactions. These may include service issues, fee waiver requests, questions asked, information requested, etc.

2. Start by gleaning what you can from the data you have. Review notes and other text-based information stored in the CRM.
3. For each contact channel, come up with a standardized way of tracking the interaction.
4. Train front line personal to recognize these interactions and note them in the account.
5. Begin to extract these data elements and include them in modeling and decision-making exercises.

A final note: new text-based analytics may make it easier to parse free text notes fields for phrases that are relevant for decision-making. Instead of having to standardize coding, soon it may only be necessary to instruct front line staff to include notes on these interactions.

If front line staff uses text to describe more and more interactions, these big data techniques can find other interactions that banks haven't even considered yet which are predictive of some kind of customer behavior. But it starts with collecting data.

So, if banks do nothing else with this information: start collecting data.

As far as a next best action system is concerned, you must have the ability to import, merge, manage, clean, and interact with these different data sets. Broadly speaking, this data management functionality must be performed—whether in a single-platform system or by stringing several different vendor tools together.

Features a bank should look for in such a data-management system include:

- Data import
- Data merge

- Data append
- Data cleansing
- Data export
- Data filtering

When a bank takes the resulting data and does something with it, of course, more functionality will be needed. But we'll continue to add to that list as we go.

METRICS

As I mentioned earlier, I'm defining a metric as a new piece of information created from source data. In the vast majority of cases, this new information wouldn't be collectible on its own.

There are three major categories of metrics for the purposes of next best action technology: key performance indicators (KPIs), behavioral outcomes, and decision objectives.

KPIs

The most general category is the KPI. Basically, a KPI is anything that your bank wants to track. Typically though, it's something by which the bank can manage a portfolio.

For a portfolio of loans, important KPIs may include such things as:

- Number of new originations
- Percent of new originations in a certain customer segment
- Percent of applications approved in underwriting
- Volume-weighted margin
- Volume-weighted losses
- Etc.

Clearly, this isn't an exhaustive list. But each of these items, if known, could trigger a decision process.

For each decision made, the bank will need a set of KPIs to guide its actions. Even if there isn't a direct relationship between the KPI and action, knowing the information may be vital to make the final decision. Thus, we calculate the KPIs necessary to fill out this list. And the calculation is derived from source data and other previously calculated KPIs. In that sense, KPIs are derived columns or summary metrics from a table or set of tables.

Behavioral Outcomes
The next category of metric is critical for the statistical portion of next best action technology. They are the behavioral outcomes. There is a relatively small list of these compared to KPIs. They may, in some cases, even be considered to be KPIs, but in the context of next best action, they are only one step on the way to optimal decision-making. But depending on the decision you are trying to make, there are specific behavioral outcomes you will want to track. A list of such behavioral outcomes is listed here. (See Figure 4.) Definitions follow.

Decision	Deposits	Loans
Marketing	• Response rate of campaign	• Response rate of campaign
Bundling	• Affinity with another product	• Affinity with another product
Pricing	• Number of accounts opened • Volume of accounts opened • Number of term deposit renewals • Volume of term deposit renewals • Volume of deposits transferred in from another account	• Number of accounts opened • Volume of accounts opened • Conversion rate from application to loan • Prepayment rate (by month) • Default rate (by month)
Servicing	• None specific	• None specific
Retention	• Number of accounts closed • Volume of accounts closed • Retention rate	• Number of accounts closed • Volume of accounts closed • Retention rate
Collection	• Number of "bad" accounts • Volume lost due to fraud • Loss rate due to fraud	• Number of delinquent accounts • Volume delinquent • Delinquency rate • Expected payment under modified conditions

Figure 4. List of Models by Decision Type

Although this list may look similar to the KPI list, these metrics are not calculated from source data; they are instead predicted statistically by the source data. They are the dependent variables in the statistical models.

We'll spend time talking about each model type and how they're built in the next section. Suffice it to say, these are the outcomes a bank is trying to measure. Notice they are all explicitly customer oriented. If a customer doesn't move that outcome, the bank doesn't track it here.

Decision Objectives

Finally, the last category of metrics is the decision objectives. These metrics are the specific values banks are looking to maximize or minimize through its decision-making.

Decision objectives are usually financial metrics, such as profit or expenses. But they can also be operational metrics, such as number of agents assigned. These metrics are the end goal of a bank's work.

Most decisions in banking are intended to maximize the lifetime value of the customer or customers a bank is studying. Profit is a tricky subject, and you could write an entire book just on understanding financial profit.

We're going to assume you have your favorite project metric picked out for the financial product you're managing, whether it be marginal or total, return on assets (ROA), risk-adjusted return on capital (RAROC), or simply net present value (NPV).

These metrics are also not calculated from the source data, but rather are stored as formulas so the system can access them and test sample output against the desired outcome. In any system, it is the formula defining the metric rather than the value itself, which is critical.

MODELS

We turn our attention next to the statistical portion of the system: behavioral models. Recall that I defined the word model as a statistical formula built to predict the outcome of customer behavior.

In the last section, I started building a series of behavioral outcome metrics that a bank might use to help measure customer reaction to the things that it does. I called those dependent variables. You can think of them as the output of the process.

The inputs to the process are the independent variables or covariates in statistical parlance. These are the things that will influence a customer's behavior and therefore predict the outcome.

Independent variables break broadly down into two main categories: those a bank can control and those it cannot control. It is those controllable variables that will become the decision variables. But we'll discuss those more later.

There are a large variety of statistical techniques used to predict dependent variables. These techniques include: regression, survival analysis, complex event processing, neural networks, partition analysis, and many, many more. While many of these techniques are used today in risk management, fraud detection, default prediction, and so forth, we're going to focus the vast majority of our time on regression analysis.

Regression is a tried and tested technique to predict behavior. Although many of these new techniques have been developed to improve performance of some of these regression models, regression still performs quite well and has the advantage of being easy to understand and replicate.

We'll spend a few minutes with each of the others.

Regression is actually a broad class of mathematical formulas. But they're all built with one idea in mind: minimize the predictive error of the formula you come up with. The differences come down to the mathematical formula you use, the way you define "predictive error," and the way you minimize it.

So while some statistician will argue with this, I'm going to lump a lot of statistical techniques together and call them a form of regression. While by no means being exhaustive, here is a short list of techniques we'll consider:

- Linear regression
- Logistic regression
- Multinomial regression
- Exponential and gamma regression

- Poisson regression
- Survival analysis

Linear Regression

Linear regression is the most common form—and the most abused—type of statistical analysis. In order for linear regression to be the right technique, the dependent variable, a customer's outcome, must be measured as a continuous number taking on all values—positive and negative. The shape of the distribution of values - a bell curve - is also vital. There are several other technical assumptions necessary to justify linear regression like the distribution of error terms, but they tend to be less abused than the type of dependent variable you use.

The most common mistake made with linear regression is to use it for outcome metrics that are only positive like loan balance or number of accounts. These are (generally) positive-only values. Because of this, the distribution of the values tend to be skewed. Therefore, linear regression is the wrong tool. There are those practitioners who argue that if the possible values are limited— like credit scores from 450–900—then for some purposes it's okay to use linear regression even though the distribution of those values isn't distributed equally around a mean.

Linear regression is an often misused tool, so my advice is to tread carefully. Banks can often make mistakes by assuming without even knowing it. It's not that hard to "do it right."

So what might you use linear regression for? You could use it to predict a bias from a published index value. For example, if you were using a published automobile value index, you might discover a bias in your portfolio's vehicle values. In that case, a linear regression can predict that bias based on your portfolio's characteristics. Bias is something that can be positive or negative and will probably be evenly distributed around the average bias.

Even though money values can be positive or negative, often money behaves like a scaled value. This behavior means that some exponential transformation makes the model fit better. Banks usually take a logarithm of money values before using them in order to adjust for this behavior. I'm not going to go into the theory as to why, but suffice it to say that as money values get bigger and bigger, they become much less likely to be observed. So much less likely, that a log transformation does a good job in correcting for that low likelihood.

If that's confusing, don't worry; it's just good to know that logs are helpful when dealing with monetary values. If logs bring back bad memories from school, don't worry; the analyst knows what they are. But, it may make a good interview question when the bank is hiring a new statistical analyst.

Linear regression is so common that you can fit the models in Microsoft Excel if you want. But my recommendation is to use a statistical package that will not only give you the regressed formula, but also the statistical measurement of that formula so you can see if you've got a good fit or not.

Logistic Regression
The next most common regression technique is logistic regression. Logistic regression is used in cases where your outcome variable is measured as a binary "yes"/"no" at the customer level. The bank may measure this as a percentage at the portfolio level, but it comes down to adding up a bunch of 1's and 0's and dividing them by the count.

This is common in customer behavior. Customers accept an offer or not. Customers open an account or not. Customers decide to stay or do not. Customers pay their bill or do not (that one is a little more complicated, and we'll discuss it later.)

Because behavior is often binary, logistic regression is a powerful technique for studying customer response. The vast majority of statistical packages support logistic regression. If the outcome is coded variable correctly—as a binary variable—then the statistical package will handle it correctly.

Depending on the package, the bank may need to transform the outcome into 0 or 1 although it may be able to leave it as two categories: yes or no, as an example. It's just important to remember that if it uses numeric values, like 0 and 1, not to code these as continuous number, or even numbers at all. They are not numbers; they are categories. Your statistical software will need to be able to tell the difference. The fundamental difference is: even though you're using 0 and 1, the value 0.5 is impossible. That difference is also the reason why—although a common mistake —it is fundamentally wrong to use linear regression to predict these 0/1 values.

Multinomial Regression

The next variant, multinomial regression, is a slight variation over logistic regression. With multinomial regression, the outcome variable is several discrete possibilities, rather than just two. So, instead of "yes" vs. "no", you might have "A" vs. "B" vs. "C."

The most common use of multinomial regression in the context of customer behavior is modeling customer choice across a number of different possible outcomes. Perhaps your bank offers three packages, A, B, and C, to a customer. Multinomial regression would predict the likelihood of choosing one of these three based on the given independent variables.

One other common mistake used here is when the variable used for these choices take on numeric values. Let's say the packages are called 1, 2, and 3. Some analysts may mistakenly use regression techniques that assume these are numbers like linear regression. But remember, the fact that you use numbers comes with an assumption that 2 is between 1 and 3 in some way. If the bank is offering three different packages called 1, 2, and 3, 2, it's not really "in between" 1 and 3. In fact, even if the packages are ordered in some increasing value, there is no such thing as "in between."

The moral of the story is: beware using numbers to represent discrete objects.

If you've done some basic statistics work, you may have heard of the last three regression models we've just discussed. Less often heard though is the exponential or gamma regression model.

Exponential or Gamma Regression
In the case you have an output variable which is a continuous number, but only takes on positive values, you may have a case for exponential or gamma regression. In fact, exponential regression is just a special case of gamma regression, so we'll just refer to it as gamma regression from this point on.

As with the other regression types we've discussed, there are some technical assumptions about the distribution of variables. But, as before, we'll leave those to the statisticians and say that in most cases, as long as your output variable is non-negative and continuous, gamma regression may be a good tool to try.

Banks may use gamma regression to predict account balances. This works for two reasons. First, account balances are non-negative (generally, exceptions aren't the norm, unless of course, overdraft accounts are what you're studying). Second, monetary values tend to match the theoretic distribution needed for gamma regression. Remember how we talked earlier about using log transformations for monetary values? Gamma regression builds that kind of transformation into the formula. So in some sense, the technique is built for predict monetary values.

The difference between exponential and gamma regression comes down to the selection of one parameter in the distribution of the outcome variable. Don't worry about that; let the analyst deal with it. If the exponential distribution is right, the gamma regression will turn into exponential regression.

Common uses for gamma regression in the context of customer behavior include:

- Predicting account balances (non-negative) at a particular point in time
- Predicting the current deposit balance as a proportion of the original balance (non-negative, with the mean around 1) at a particular point in time
- Predicting the current loan balance as a proportion of the original balance (non-negative, with the mean lower than 1) after 12 months
- Predicting the opening balance of a new loan taken out as the result of an offer made (non-negative)
- Predicting the amount of the next payment sent in during collections when the customer cannot afford their full payment (non-negative)

- Predicting the amount of the next payment sent in during collections expressed as a proportion of the original payment (non-negative, skewing left from 1)

You can see some of these examples are better than others. They're better because the distribution is more stable. When all customers are normalized together so their behavior can be measured on the same scale, you get better prediction. That's why examples that predict proportions are more stable, because every customer is normalized to 1.

Check the statistics package to see if it supports gamma regression. It's common to see people mistakenly use linear regression here. But remember, if the value you're predicting can't go negative, chances are, you cannot use a linear technique. Gamma will often fit better.

Many decisions cannot effectively be made without gamma regression. For example, understanding the lifetime profitability of a line of credit, credit card, or deposit account over time will require some prediction of future monetary values. These models will require some kind of gamma regression to accurately predict.

Many banks that have not built these models have developed assumptions around line utilization, credit utilization, or balance growth in order to compensate. It's fine to start off with these assumptions, but in order to make personalized and individual decisions, model these things at the customer level. Gamma regression is the tool.

Poisson Regression

Poisson regression is less often used, but it's still a very important tool when the customer behavior a bank is measuring can be expressed as a (non-negative) count. For example, the bank may want to predict the number of accounts a customer will open. Or it may want to predict the number of times a customer will visit the branch. Or it may want to predict the number of people in line at any particular time. Each of these examples is something that Poisson regression can help with.

There are also specific examples of Poisson regression modeling the rate of an observation, where the numerator is the count of observations and the denominator is some "exposure" or measurement frame. An example of this might be predicting the market size of the bank in different cities. Count the number of customers in the city (the numerator of the fraction) and the "exposure" here is the population of the city (the denominator of the fraction). That population size would be included in the Poisson regression as an offset.

That "exposure" framework may put time in the denominator. And in that case, Poisson regression turns into a special kind of model,[16] which belongs to a class of survival analysis.

Survival Analysis

Survival analysis is the last category of regression we'll discuss. Survival analysis is a type of analysis borrowed from the insurance world. In life and pension actuarial analysis, it's important to predict the survival rate of a population at every time period in the future. Life actuarial tables are the result of this kind of analysis.

In banking, we don't study "death" per se. But things do survive and "die": balances. In the special cases where a bank is measuring an ever-declining amount, it has survival analysis. The

---

[16] It becomes a proportional hazards model, which is one of the most powerful types of survival analysis, but whose construction is beyond the scope of this book.

way to think about this is that the population is a bunch of money, and it survives at a particular rate into the future.

The strongest example of such analysis is in collections. The monthly payment of a loan starts off at 100%. If the loan is in distress, perhaps less and less of that payment will come in month after month.

We discussed this specific example earlier when we talked about collections. When a bank makes a modification offer, it's often helpful to predict the likelihood of that new payment coming in as a survival model, with the likelihood decreasing every passing month.

Other examples include default and prepayment analysis, where the balance of the original loan "survives" from month to month.

The outcome of such analysis is that the bank can predict the proportion of payment received or balance remaining at any point in the future. Notice that this is different from other money-based analyses like gamma regression where the analysis required banks to pick a point in the future and predict the value there.

One example of this difference is in credit risk modeling for defaults. The common way to measure the probability of default is to pick the event being default after 12 months. Then measure the likelihood of the loan being in default after 12 months.

The advantage of survival analysis is that a bank can predict the likelihood of the loan being in default *at every month*, not just after 12 months.

This advantage has another nice benefit. Because a bank is measuring the potential for the "death" of the loan at any time in the future, it can use all loan data—no matter how "young"—to do this analysis. Traditionally, it would have to wait until loans are 12 months old to see if they have defaulted or not. But because survival analysis uses information even at month 1, brand new loans can be used in the analysis, which is helpful in markets where customer behavior is changing quickly.

Because survival analysis is a very particular type of regression, the data structure required for the analysis is different than other regression types. Survival analysis supports a concept called *censoring*. Censoring is where data is used, but it's only useful up to a certain point in time.

To understand the concept of censoring, think about studying patients in a pharmaceutical study where the drug is treating a deadly disease. If a patient stops coming in for visits, you know they survived up until the time they stopped coming, but no further information is available. Instead of throwing out that data, use it until the time the patient stopped coming. After that, it is censored.

In the context, the bank measures the performance of loans. It runs an analysis of loans and loans that are performing, but only 3 months old have survived 3 months. What happens after that? The bank doesn't know, but it can still use the information; it's just censored.

Because censoring the data must be formatted in such a way that the bank either knows the loan's "death date" or its "censoring date." Often, data is structured with the following columns:

- Loan and customer characteristics (multiple columns)
- Stop time
- Censoring type

All loans have a stop time; they either default or you stop observing. The censoring type changes based on what happened. Censoring type is just a flag, but pay attention to the statistical software instructions to know how to set the flag. Sometimes 0 means censor; sometimes 1 does. Ask your vendor.

The output of this analysis is a "vector" or a set of probabilities at every time period in the future that the loan "dies" —whatever that means in the context of your analysis. Those vectors can easily be translated into default and prepayment assumptions. They can also be used in collections to predict the survivability of a loan modification.

Other Analytic Techniques

I don't want to spend too much more time on analytic techniques because the remainder are either very new or very specialized. We've discussed complex event processing as a way of detecting customer behavior based on a series of preceding events. CEP is so unique and specialized that you will likely need to find a vendor that focuses in this area.

All I want to say is that CEP is a powerful technique to predict individual behavior and will likely become a core analytic technique to prepare for retention, collections, and other important events in the lifecycle of the customer.

Another analytic technique involves neural networks, which are complex algorithms used to predict outcomes. The idea is that a learning infrastructure is mimicked, much like the brain would learn, by a set of nodes which encode information about how input information is transformed into output information. The algorithm iterates, each time improving the fit until no further improvement is possible or practical.

The fundamental problem with most neural networks is the lack of transparency on how the thing works. Many regulatory agencies have expressed concern about the use of neural networks in credit-risk analysis because the analyst cannot explicitly point out how an input variable affects the output. That criticism remains even after considering that in some cases, neural networks outperform regression analysis.

Neural networks are used extensively in data processing, signals controls, and classifications. Lately, robotics has had success integrating neural network processing into manipulating prostheses. Electronic applications include classification of email as spam and mining knowledge out of databases, such as e-discovery in a legal context.

It may be the case in the future that neural networks will become a key part of customer behavior analysis. The problem in banking, however, is not a problem of analytic technique; it's a problem of data usage. We will likely make much more progress toward personalization of the banking experience by collecting and using customer data than by using high-powered analytic techniques.

But that could change.

Finally, I'll give a word on partition analysis. Recursive partitioning, as it's otherwise known, is a statistical technique that gives rise to a decision tree. Input variables decide which branch to go down and the leaves determine the end result.

Decision trees are used extensively in banking, especially for credit decision-making. Most of these trees, however, are not the result of recursive partitioning. Instead, they are the result of rules put in place by decision makers. The decision tree, in this case, is simply the automation of the knowledge of the decision maker, rather than an analytic output.

In the case, however, where analytics is used to build the decision tree, the partition analysis can be used to find a prediction of a particular model.

Decision trees—as the name implies—are best used for decisions. Decisions are typically discrete in nature and therefore, they can be well modeled with a tree. If the decision the bank is trying to make, or if the value it is trying to predict is continuous, decision trees are a very bad choice of tool.

Many decision-making vendors trying to set pricing will use a decision tree to set a continuous variable output. They do this because they are reusing a tool they already have in their toolbox. But it is often as effective as using a flat-head screwdriver for a Phillips-head screw. You can do it, but it's much more effective to use the right tool.

Decision trees can also have the danger of overfitting data. This is especially the case where the decision tree is predicting a variable rather than making a decision. Decisions can often be less sensitive to overfitting than customer behavior can.

On the other hand, decision trees have the benefit of allowing the user to tweak them—pruning and splitting nodes at will to get the desired output. My feeling is that this habit of manually manipulating decision trees is to compensate for the fact that the infrastructure is wrong, the data is not robust enough, or the decision tree itself is the wrong tool.

Chapter 9. The Execution of Next Best Action: The Decisions

Now that we've covered a number of different ways of predicting customer behavior, we'll move onto the final act: making a personalized decision that maximizes a customer's lifetime value while staying true to the goals of the organization.

Decisions don't get a lot of attention in analytic frameworks, but they are the end goal. In fact, I would argue that an analytic system is built specifically to generate a decision. Often, those decisions are made by bankers' gut feelings, but they are made (hopefully) with some data, metrics, and if we're really lucky, models behind them.

But we can do better, much better.

Decisions are the reason banks have analytics. Any analytic exercise that doesn't lead to a decision is a wasted one. Now, those decisions may be informed by the analytics rather than directed by them, but either way, we need to make decisions.

In the new personalized banking experience, the decisions need to be individual ones. The bank needs to make an individual decision for each customer at each touch point and each interaction that answers the question: what should I do next that will maximize the lifetime value of this customer and is in line with the corporate goals?

If it sounds like an impossibility, it is not. Systems exist today that can provide this functionality. The missing piece is organizational commitment to implement them, which means gathering data, deciding on metrics, and building the appropriate models.

As a shortcut, I'm going to start calling the individual decision that maximizes customer lifetime value while being consistent with organizational goals as an *optimal decision*. Optimal can mean a lot of things to a lot of people, but from here on, when I use it, that's what I mean.

Behind optimal decision-making there are four parts:

- The trigger
- The decision variable
- The objective
- The business rules

We'll cover all four in detail so you can see how they come together on a day-to-day basis in the bank.

THE TRIGGER

The trigger is the event that kicks off an analysis to make a decision. In some cases, this is obvious. When a customer asks for a price quote, the bank makes a decision. When a customer explains why they're closing their account, we make a decision.

In many cases, however, the trigger is not so obvious. In the framework of next best action, the idea is that every moment is a potential trigger for a decision, even if the customer isn't interacting with his bank. Remember those push alerts in our mobile app?

But just a framework isn't practical. We have to narrow down the lifecycle of the customer into triggers we can manage.

Here are several triggers your bank probably manages today and a few that it should be managing:

- Request a rate quote
- Submit an application
- Open an account
- Make a large deposit
- Make a large withdrawal
- Change account information (such as address)
- Submit a complaint
- Mention the bank on social media
- Spend (significantly) more than average during a month
- Spend (significantly) less than average during a month
- Interact with contact center
- Visit the branch
- Receive a monthly statement
- Pay a bill late
- Request to close an account
- Request a fee waiver
- Visit the website to research a product
- Log into online banking
- Check the mobile app for a balance
- Add a new payee on bill pay
- Start using bill pay
- Stop using bill pay
- Visit the ATM

Obviously this is just the beginning of a list. And keep in mind that if your bank uses complex event processing (CEP), it can actually create a series of events which in of and themselves become a trigger.

It doesn't matter if some of these triggers don't end up triggering some kind of action. The idea is that the trigger kicks off an evaluation process to find the next best action. The next best action may in fact be "do nothing."

Most of the bank's time will be spent in finding good triggers. In fact, designing the right personalized experience will be all about creating and decision-making off the right triggers. Spend time here testing and learning from what customers do. They speak loudest with their pocketbooks, their actions.

THE DECISION VARIABLE

It's a bit of a misnomer to talk about the (singular) decision variable. In fact, there are many decision variables. But the idea is that the decision variable is the thing that you are deciding right now.

That decision may be what action to take. It may be which program to offer. And if the bank is offering a program, it may be at which terms to offer the program.

Banks will be making multiple decisions—some in series, some in parallel. The sequence and timing of those decisions is called the *choice architecture.* For each interaction with the customer, the bank needs to first design and diagram the choice architecture. It helps them understand what decisions they're making and when.

Let's take the example of making a direct marketing credit card offer. Say you've got an existing customer and some trigger kicks the process off. Let's say he is on the website looking at financial products. The process may look something like this. (See Figure 5.)

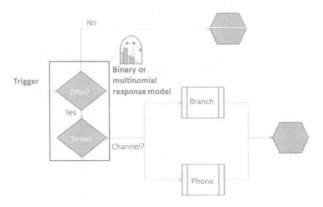

Figure 5. Choice Architecture for Direct Marketing

The trigger kicks off two decisions in series. First, do you even make an offer to the person? If no, then the process stops and nothing happens. If yes, then you have another decision: what are the terms of the offer? Then after that, you may have to decide if you communicate the offer? Via branch or phone?

This could clearly be even more complex. What if it's not just credit cards, but all financial products? Now there's a decision to choose the product and terms. But these two decisions will need to happen simultaneously because you don't know what will be most profitable until you know the terms of the offer.

Some banks pick the product first, then choose the terms. But this choice architecture will always be suboptimal though it may be required.

So there is a hierarchy of decision variables. At the top of the hierarchy is the decision variable: take action. It is binary: "yes" or "no."

Right below that is a collection of actions. This set of actions is called the *action space*. That's a technical term, but it basically means it's all the actions that are under consideration for this customer.

The action space may include things like:

- Make a product offer
- Make a pricing decision
- Make a servicing offer (e.g., signing up for electronic statements, etc.)
- Make a retention offer (e.g., waive a fee, etc.)
- Make a collections offer (e.g., negotiate a settlement on a late payment, etc.)

Not all of these actions will be valid for all customers at all times. Obviously, if a customer doesn't have a late loan or is in danger of having a late loan, then those actions aren't applicable.

You can see that a bank could end up with a very large action space if it's not careful. But by using a simple framework, you can actually break down most of what you do into classifications. These five categories correspond to five critical moments that truly matter in the lifecycle of the customer.

From here, it can drill down into types of actions, terms and conditions of those actions, and so forth. That drill-down path will depend on each action's choice architecture. Designing that choice architecture is important because it will become the framework for how to solve the problem. Make sure that whatever system you develop to handle next best action technology can adjust based on that choice architecture.

One last point on decision variables: we have been discussing decision variables that affect customer behavior today at the moment of decision. There is the possibility, however, of making a decision today knowing that in the future the bank will have the ability to make other decisions that will affect the customer lifetime value.

For example, it may offer a deposit product with a fee waiver today knowing that in a year it will be able to sell a credit card with a slightly higher rate because they now have an existing customer. Banks try to guess these dynamics when they use loss leader pricing, but if they have the data and the models, they can actually make these decisions using analytics.

In order to do this, however, they will have to have a model that predicts future behavior from customers based on the decision you make today. That future predicting model will then be fed into a decision engine which selects not only what offer the bank makes today, but what offer it's likely to make in the future given what it does today.

This kind of multi-period decisioning is cutting edge in banking. It has application in a number of areas. We've just covered an example from marketing, but clearly there are examples from retention and collections as well. Treating a customer one way today will definitely have impact in the future.

For today, just know the possibility is out there and start collecting the data to build these future-predicting models. Then your bank will be able to make very sophisticated decisions, personalized for each customer today and the future.

THE OBJECTIVE

All decisions need to have an objective. In mathematics, this is called the *objective function*. It doesn't have to be that formal though. Banks are driven by profit. Clearly not profit over all other considerations, but profit as a tie-breaker.

So when we define the objective, it's maximizing the customer's lifetime value, which is closely related to profit. Based on the scope of the decision the bank is trying to make, and frankly, the quality of data available, it may define the objective in a very short-term way: margin for a new loan or deposit product.

But remember that being too short sighted can be a problem. So keep a bank must keep its "eyes" wide open to whatever objective it chooses.

To have an objective useful for decision-making, the bank will create a formula for profit or lifetime value at the customer level. This formula will involve the behavioral model formulas already defined; if it didn't, then the customers' profits would be unrelated to what they do, which doesn't make any sense.

Generally speaking, we are looking for some kind of expected profit or expected value function. The pattern looks like this:

Probability of occurrence * Profit if it does occur

Each of those factors will have a number of behavioral components. The probability will almost exclusively be a behavioral model. The profit will also contain behavioral components. For example, profit on loans will contain behavior for default and prepayment. Profit on lines of credits and credit cards will also contain behavior around line utilization. Profit on deposits will assume some kind of balance growth or decline. These are all behavioral components.

What about complex business scenarios where the bank has more than one objective? Say it wants to grow the business, but do so profitably? If it gains market, it does so at the expense of profit? Does it have two objectives?

There is a special way of handling these trade-offs called *Pareto* or *multi-objective optimization*. Basically it generates a number of scenarios where the bank sets all but one of the objectives to a set value and maximize the remaining objective given the ones that are fixed.

So in the case I just described, the bank would pick a volume target and maximize profit under that scenario. But it could choose the other way; pick a profit target and maximize volume under that scenario.

It gets a little more complicated when you have more than two objectives, but the idea is the same. Let's say your bank wanted to trade off volume, profit, and a weighted-average loss rate. It would generate a number of scenarios where it picked a volume target, a weighted-average loss rate target, and maximize profit under those circumstances. Now repeat a lot of times.

When you plot all of these different scenarios on a graph, you get an efficient frontier: the boundary beyond which it's not possible to find a scenario. (See Figure 6.)

You can see from the graph that the curve acts as a strategic planning tool. You can see where banks are today (under the curve) and decide where banks want to go (to the curve). In this case, they have several options including keeping their existing profit and increasing volume. This would correspond to the spot vertically up from the dot. Or, they could keep their existing volume and increase profit. This would correspond to the spot horizontally right from the dot. And there may be a number of scenarios that do a little of both.

Figure 6. Tradeoff between Profit and Volume

This strategic planning isn't a math problem; it's literally a conversation the bank has to decide what its strategic objectives should be.

Notice this is a bit backwards from the standard operating procedure where strategic objectives are set in advance and then the banks has to figure out how to achieve them. Here, we see what's achievable and choose the scenario we want.

Many banks have found this conversation allows them to reject strategic plans that cannot be achieved or realize potential that they didn't even know existed.

But it does translate strategic plans made at the top of the organization into customer-by-customer actions meant to achieve those objectives. This process is the way that a bank executes on a personalized and individual strategy, but still achieves its goals.

THE BUSINESS RULES

The thing that makes optimal decision-making work is that it conforms to your business rules. Business rules are goals you have to achieve which are not explicitly objectives. Often, we use the term constraint interchangeably with business rule. Granted, there is a bit of a fuzzy line between a constraint and an objective.

For example, the constraint may be that you need to achieve a certain weighted-average loss rate. But, if you are willing to be flexible on that number, but need to control it, you might make it an objective so you can see multiple options. The difference is that a constraint is a goal you hit.

There are three major categories of business rules:

1. Eligibility rules
2. Boundary values
3. Global constraints

Eligibility Rules
Eligibility rules are requirements placed on which broad decision a customer is eligible for. We already saw that not all customers need to be considered for the five key moments. In turn, not all customers are eligible for your entire action space.

By setting good eligibility criteria, you have immediately reduced the size of the problem. Decisions can be made faster and more efficiently with a robust set of eligibility criteria.

The downside of eligibility rules is that they can be misused. Many rules which are used to keep people out of program are really not hard and fast; they are simply rules that were used to approximate what business owners thought was right. In other words, they were the decisioning criteria.

As you review the rule set you're working from, make sure you can justify that eligibility rules are truly that - hard and fast rules that determine if someone should qualify or not.

For example, a customer with no loan products cannot be eligible for a collections program. That is an obvious eligibility rule.

A customer with a low credit score may not be eligible for a credit card. If that cutoff is hard and fast, it also is an eligibility rule.

But a customer with a low credit score may be eligible for a credit card with a higher interest rate. The line between the decline and the price is a fuzzy one. Make sure you've chosen it for a reason. We'll discuss that a bit more later when we talk about risk management.

Boundary Values

Boundary values are special rules that apply to decision variables which are numeric. The obvious example is price. If you are choosing the right price for a customer, that price will have an upper bound and a lower bound.

Another example is a fee. You may decide to allow a cash management fee to be different for each commercial customer. In that case, you also will have a lower and an upper bound.

Any numeric decision variable should have boundary values.

Global Constraints

The most interesting kind of constraint, though, is the global constraint. Here is where the true power of optimal decisions is achieved.

Let's say that you are interested in pricing term deposits. You have several goals. First, you want to achieve maximal profit; this is your objective. Next, you want to control for project balances; this is a secondary objective and you'll draw a trade-off graph between the two.

But let's say in addition, treasury demands that the new term deposit portfolio have a volume-weighted average life of 12 months. Today, your weighted average life is 10 months. So you will need to encourage some longer term deposits. But how? What pricing strategy will achieve all of these goals together?

By using a global constraint on the volume weighted-average life of the total final portfolio, you can be sure that the optimal decision you are looking for will include the projection of a 12-month weighted average life - if such a thing is possible.

Of course, that's the trick. You can place all sorts of constraints on the problem, but if it's not possible, there will be no answer. Thus you have to be careful with constraints.

Constraints will do three things: two bad and one good. First, they will make the problem harder (and therefore it'll take longer to solve.) The only exception is a set of eligibility rules. Second, they will not increase your objective - and in fact, might even decrease it. Adding rules never adds to your profit objective. And in fact, you may eat away at profit by doing that. And that's even true with eligibility rules.

But lastly, a good set of constraints makes the output of your problem useable. So it's like spices in cooking. You need some to make dish taste good. Use too much and you spoil the whole meal.

An Optimal Decisioning System

There are many vendors who offer decision making systems to banks. I suspect given the nature of analytics that list will only grow over time.

This book is not intended to be a vendor selection guide; I'll leave that to others. But do consider the following requirements when considering a vendor:

- Support the data-management needs of merging different data sources.
- Support metric construction not just through calculated columns but by the creation and storage of formulas.
- Support model building through a transparent framework to build and calculate the different model types which we've discussed and are relevant to your problem.
- Support optimal decision-making by allowing for multiple objectives and constraints.
- Support on-going decision-making by integrating into front line systems that are responsible for delivering the decision result to the marketplace.

As you look at different vendor options, you'll see strengths and weaknesses in several of these areas. Think through your enterprise carefully. The right solution may be a mix of vendor support and internal effort. But make that decision actively rather than finding out your choice leaves you unsupported in your path to developing a personalized, profitable banking experience for your customers.

CHAPTER 10. EXAMPLES OF OPTIMAL DECISION-MAKING

We've spent a lot of time in the theory of decision-making. I want to make things fairly concrete by outlining some examples. I will talk through those examples in the framework of data, metrics, models, and decisions that we've described so far. Hopefully, they will make the theory more understandable.

They are not intended to represent all possible ways this technology can be used. I hope as you read each example, you think broadly about your bank and how these cases can be applied.

MARKETING

Scenario: A visitor comes to your website to apply for a credit card. You want to suggest the right card and terms for the individual.

Trigger: A visitor to your website applies for a card.

Data: Since this is not a customer, you only have information provided in the browser cookies. (Depending on your geography this may or may not be effective.) Additional information can be purchased through marketing vendors. Or, worst-case scenario, start the application early before the offer is made.

Metrics: The key metric here is customer profitability. This would be a pro forma profit calculation that most likely takes customer defaults and credit utilization forecasts into consideration.

Models: The primary model will be the customer's response model predicting the probability of acceptance of an offer. The independent variables will be the credit card type and the terms of the office (interest rate and credit limit).

Additionally, other models needed include risk models for credit default and line utilization based on the assigned credit limit.

Decision: There are 4 decisions that need to be made.

1. Do you offer anything at all?
2. What type of credit card do you offer? (e.g. rewards, travel card, etc.)
3. What interest rate do you offer?
4. What credit limit do you offer?

The variable types of these decisions are:

1. binary: "yes"/"no"
2. categorical: "A" vs. "B" vs. "C"
3. continuous: with minimum and maximum
4. categorical: there are specific credit limits offered

The last one might be confusing. The credit limit is a number, but you aren't going to set credit limits at every one of those continuous values like $3,517. You have very particular offers; those are categorical.

The objective will be expected profit for each prospect:

Probability of acceptance * Profitability of Credit Card

Constraints will include eligibility rules for each credit card offer. Also, the interest rate will be constrained with a maximum and minimum interest rate. Finally, there may be a constraint that ensures a minimum number of new credit cards opened.

You may ask, how can you have a global constraint when we are making a decision on just one prospect? The answer is in the tradeoff graph we looked at earlier. The selection of a spot on that graph comes with an implicit tradeoff between getting the customer to say yes and getting profit from the deal. That balance can be reflected with each prospect, and over time, you will reach your goals.

PRICING

Scenario: The deposits pricing committee sets the rate sheet for savings and term deposit products.

Trigger: Competitors have changed their deposit rates and/or the overall interest rate environment has changed.

Data: Here you have an entire history of customer balances. Take balances of each type of product over time. Collect the banks and your competitors' rates over the same period.

Metrics: The major metrics here are the number of new accounts, the amount of new money, and perhaps the amount of money being withdrawn. Finally, the key metric will be profitability on the future balance. Perhaps it could be something as simple as the margin of earnings credit net interest rate paid out.

Models: The primary model is a forecast of balances by deposit product. The dependent variable is the total balance of each product at some point in the future. The independent variables include your interest rate, your competitors' interest rates, and the macroeconomic conditions. Depending on your data and product structure, you may also want to include rates of similar products to measure the cannibalization effect due to having two products' rate too close together.

Decisions: There are several decision variables. In particular, one interest rate for every cell on your rate sheet. That may be broken out by product type, term of term deposit, and balance tier. There may be other breakouts as well. These are all numeric variables bounded by a maximum and minimum interest rate.

The objective is projected profit based on the margin metric we just discussed.

Constraints do not include any eligibility rules here since we're not making decisions at the customer level, but instead at a rate sheet level. But they definitely include bounds on all rates on the rate sheet.

There is a unique type of constraint involved with rate sheet pricing: relative pricing. The rate is one cell cannot be priced independently of the other cells. In fact, a bank may have strict rules about one cell being higher or lower than another. Or being higher by at least 10 basis points. These relative pricing rules can be complex, but critical to creating a good rate sheet.

Finally, there may be a global constraint that requires a certain balance in each cell. That constraint will balance the need for profit against the need for new money.

SERVICING

Scenario: When a customer is out with his mobile device, the bank decides whether to send a discount offer via push alert for a store he happens to be near.

Recall that our definition of servicing is everything from account opening to account closing. So this is an example of servicing even though it doesn't sound like it.

Trigger: The customer is near a participating merchant as detected by the mobile banking application on the customer's phone.

Data: The data here will be a history of offers made to customers at different merchants. The data set will include customers' transaction history, the discount offer made, the store it was made at, and a record of whether the customer used that discount.

Metrics: The key metric here will be the profitability of the transaction including the discount. That may include both interchange fee and discount rate for the merchant.

Models: The model here is the probability that the customer will accept the discount offer and make a purchase. The independent variables will be the transaction history of the customer including whether or not the customer has purchased at this merchant before, how often, how much, etc.

Decisions: There are two major decisions variables here:

1. Do you make an offer?
2. What discount do you offer?

The first decision is binary: "yes" vs. "no." The second decision is numeric and continuous, bounded by a maximum and minimum.

The objective will be the expected profit of the transaction:

Probability of accepting the discount * Profit on transaction

There will be eligibility criteria potentially based on the customer's history. Perhaps a customer needs to buy a certain amount from a merchant in order to qualify. The discount is a numeric variable with boundary constraints. And you may have a global constraint that ensures a certain number of discount transactions as an agreement with the merchant. That would trade off the profitability of the transaction with the number of expected transactions.

RETENTION

Scenario: You recognize a pattern of behavior in your customer's credit card transactions that makes you think he may be ready to close his account. The bank needs to decide what to do, if anything, to retain the customer.

Trigger: Here the trigger is a series of events: the customer pays off the balance, stops transacting on the card for 60 days, and you detect monthly bill payment to another bank for two months.

Data: The data you use is the history of customers with this type of credit card and the retention offers you've made. The data file contains customer demographics, transaction history, the type of offer, the amount of the offer, and the result, whether the customer stayed or not.

Metrics: The key metric is going to be the profitability of the customer's credit card account. This will include expected defaults and line utilization forecasts based on expected usage after the retention offer is made.

Models: The primary customer behavior model is whether the customer stays or closes his account. The independent variables include the type of retention offer made and its amount. Another model will be necessary that forecasts the utilization of the credit card after the specific retention offer has been made.

Decisions: There are three decision variables involved:

1. Do you make an offer at all?

2. What type of retention offer should you make?
3. What offer should you make?

The decision variable types are as follows:

1. Binary "yes" vs. "no"
2. Categorical: "A" vs. "B" vs. "C." (perhaps a credit limit increase vs. a discounted interest rate)
3. Continuous numeric with boundaries

The objective is to calculate the expected profitability. Now, in this case, there is the possibility that the customer doesn't leave at all. So the objective looks like this:

Probability of staying with no offer * Profitability of current account +

Probability of staying with an offer * Profitability of account with new offer

Constraints will include eligibility rules for each of the retention offers. For example, you may not want to offer a credit line increase if the customer has paid late on his bill in the last six months. Also include boundary values on the amount of the offer.

Finally, you may have global constraints that ensure a minimum retention percentage of credit card customers. This global constraint would balance the goal for profitability in these accounts with the goal for having a low-churn number.

COLLECTIONS

Scenario: A customer is 90-days late on his mortgage. You need to decide how to handle the collection effort.

Trigger: The customer is 90-days late.

Data: The data is the history of all collection efforts of this type. It includes the loan information, customer characteristics, the collection treatment offers, and the result of the offer—whether successful or unsuccessful.

Metrics: Here, you want to consider the net present value of cash flow for this customer going forward after the collection treatment has been applied.

Models: The primary behavioral model is a survival model that projects forward the "survival" of payments into the future. The independent variables include the collection treatment offered and the terms of the offer.

In this data set, you will consider all loans 90 days past due. Some of those loans will be performing after collection and some will not. You can build a survival model off this data by setting the last period of observation as the final stopped payment after collection efforts or the month of the analysis. Those loans that are still performing are censored for the survival analysis.

Decisions: There are two major decision variables here:

1. What kind of collection treatment do you offer?
2. What are the terms and conditions of that treatment?

The first decision variable is categorical: do nothing, modify, negotiate, etc. The second decision variable is a continuous numeric with bounded values for maximums and minimums.

The objective will be the expected net present value of cash flow. That looks like this:

Sum of: (Probability of receiving future payment * Future payment as part of the treatment) / Discount Factor

Constraints will include eligibility criteria for each of the collections programs. It will also include boundaries for any of the numeric variables. You may also have global constraints that ensure a certain cash flow in a short period of time. That global constraint may trade off more profitable modifications that collect money over a longer period of time in favor of shorter0term one-time settlements, which bring cash today.

ENTERPRISE NEXT BEST ACTION

Scenario: The bank looks across all different actions it could take in order to decide the enterprise next best action. The action space available for this customer is to offer a credit card, encourage the customer to opt into electronic statements, offer the customer a retention offer to keep his deposit account, or collect on an overdue account.

Trigger: The user logs into his online banking application from a home computer.

Data: This is a combination of all the different decision problems we've discussed. The data will be for credit card offers, electronic statement offers, retention offers, and collection negotiations.

Metrics: The metrics necessary here are the combinations of all of the metrics necessary for all the other decisions. They will include profitability of a new credit card account for this customer, the cost savings of replacing paper statements with electronic statements, the revenue saved due to a retention offer, and new cash flow generated from a collection negotiation.

Models: There are multiple models involved. It includes a behavioral model that measures the probability of accepting the credit card offer, a model that predicts the likelihood this customer will opt into electronic statements, a model that predicts the likelihood—given the current transactions —that this customer is in danger of churning, and a model that predicts the probability this customer will respond to a collection treatment and in turn the cash it would generate.

Also, the profitability models related to each product are required.

Decisions: There are many decision variables here:

1. Do you act at all?
2. What offer do you make: credit card, e-statements, retention, or collections?
3. If a credit card, which card and which terms?
4. If a retention treatment, which offer and under which terms?
5. If a collections treatment, which collection treatment and under what terms?

They are complex and many. We won't go through each one. Clearly, the objective is the long-term profitability of this customer as expressed by the following:

Probability of accepting credit card offer * Profitability of new credit card +
Probability of accepting e-statement offer + Profitability of new e-statement delivery +
Probability of retention offer + Profitability gained based on new retention offer +
Probability of collections offer + Profitability given successful collection treatment offer

The problem lives and dies on good eligibility rules. For example:

1. If the customer already has a credit card, they are not eligible for a new credit card offer.
2. If the customer does not have any loans in danger of default, they are not eligible for a collection treatment offer.
3. If the customer already has electronic statement, then they are not eligible for an e-statements offer.
4. If the customer does not have any triggers that indicate churn,

Of course all numeric decision variables will have minimums and maximums associated with them.

Global constraints can take a unique turn here. Above the global constraints associated with each of the marketing, servicing, retention, and collections campaigns, there may be an overall constraint about how many of each thing can be offered. For example, there may be a goal to sign up a certain number of people to electronic statements. That goal may need to be emphasized over other profit goals from the other campaigns.

One thing you'll notice about structuring enterprise decision-making is that the goals need to be crafted above all lines of business—at the top of the organization. Many banks are currently not organized to agree on such tradeoffs.

Those days must end, however. Banks will need to organize themselves soon to make decisions across all lines of business at the customer level. If this industry cannot make this transformation, it will be beat by alternative players like Google, Amazon, and Paypal who do not have silos in the same way. They are organized to optimize the customer relationship at the enterprise level. It's just a matter of time.

PART IV: WHO SHOULD BANKS BE?

The third and final pillar of our bank of the future is innovative financial products. Recall that we're talking about products that meet a customer's need, not innovative financial risk hedging or something focused on internal bank needs.

Yes, you could argue that by shifting the risk of mortgage-loan origination to someone else in the mid-2000's, it allowed the bank to make more loans and thus opened up capital to customers and *that* met their needs. But I would argue that 2008–2009 would prove you wrong.

So, if we're not developing sophisticated derivatives, what are we developing?

Good question.

Fundamentally, financial products haven't changed all that much over the last several decades. Sure, banks have gotten better at pushing information through digital channels, but the core banking products are almost identical. In fact, they're almost identical from bank to bank.

So what is an innovative financial product?

It is one that meets a previously unmet customer financial need and does so in a personal way. Getting there requires thinking about the future and aiming for where the industry is going.

Wayne Gretzky, the world famous hockey player, once said:

> *"A good hockey player plays where the puck is.*
> *A great hockey player plays where the puck is going to be."*

This section will answer the following questions:
1. How can banks detect unmet customer needs?
2. How do they deploy a financial product that meets those previously unmet needs in an individual way?

CHAPTER 11. UNMET CUSTOMER NEEDS

The key to developing financial products of the future is to know what customers want...or will want. Of course, innovation is not just about asking customers what they want and then giving it to them. That often is not enough, or worse fails completely.

But customers do say the things they expect from their banks that are not currently being met. In a recent research report,[17] the management consulting and audit firm EY suggested there were three major things that banks need to start doing today.

1. Make banking clear and simple.
2. Help customers make the right financial decisions in a complex environment.
3. Work with customers when problems arise and become their advocate.

Each of these areas is woefully underrepresented in the projects that banks undertake. In fact, some may argue that banks put barriers up instead.

But it's clear that customers are asking for advice and help. Or at least they're claiming their banks aren't giving it.

We've spent quite a bit of time talking about how to reconstruct the banking experience to be clear and simple. Clear, in the sense the customer knows what he's getting and how to get it. Simple,

---

[17] "Winning through customer experience," EY Global Consumer Banking Survey 2014

in the sense the customer doesn't have to work too hard to find things. But more than that, banks can create products that make things clear and simple as well.

Consider the second item, making decisions in a complex environment. Isn't that what we've been discussing this entire book? That means the entire analytic framework for next best action that banks use to improve the profitability of their relationships could just as easily be applied to customers' financial lives to improve that financial performance as well.

Finally, let's have a discussion about advocacy. Too often customers think that when something goes wrong with their financial life, it's them versus their bank. What if your bank flipped that around? What if when payments started coming late or overdrafts started happening, instead of getting angry collection calls or terse fee announcements in the mail, they got an offer of assistance?

That would be a game changer. So let's dive in.

MAKING BANKING CLEAR AND SIMPLE

The need for clarity and simplicity is so stark that there's even a bank called Simple[18] out there. A recent survey by a major North American bank found that a paltry 6% of US consumers feel their bank or credit union makes banking simpler and easier to use.[19]

These terms, clarity and simplicity, are hardly clear and simple themselves. But for the purposes of our discussion, I want to define them in our context.

---

[18] I know Simple was acquired by BBVA in 2014, but they're still using the name.
[19] "TD Bank Checking Experience Index," TD Bank, September 2013.

When the steps to complete a process are presented in a way that they're more likely to be understood and accomplished, they are clearer.

When the steps to complete a process are reduced (i.e., fewer clicks or fewer steps), they are simpler.

Clear and simple comes down to improving the customer experience and creating new products that completely transform the process. In a recent research report[20] by Bain & Company, they summarized the issue as follows:

> *"...success hinges on making digital channels convenient and defect-free."*

They mention digital channels specifically, but the sentiment is true across the board. Regardless of how customers choose to interact with their banks, the bank needs to make the process better. The very least it can do is make it problem free, but convenience is required as well.

Achievement of clear and simple banking comes in four important stages:

1. Fix the problems.
2. Make it understandable.
3. Make it fast.
4. Transform it to a value-add.

Fix the Problems

We don't need to spend a lot of time here, do we? The problem is, banks don't spend a lot of time here. They end up with

---

[20] "Customer loyalty in retail banking: Global edition 2013," Report, Bain & Company

problems in their processes that remain unfixed. This isn't for a lack of testing; it's for a lack of customer engagement.

Think about customer touch points and ask yourself, can the customer provide feedback if there's a problem? I don't mean satisfaction scores; I mean, there's a bug and it needs fixing.

One-question surveys at the end of a call don't provide the insight a bank needs; it needs immediate feedback. Think about Android mobile applications. When they crash, you can immediately send feedback to the developer. If you do nothing but push "send," the developer is aware there's a problem and it sent relevant information to help fix the problem. If you choose to, you can add more information to provide context. But even if you don't, with one click, the feedback is sent.

Imagine if banking processes worked the same way. One "click" feedback would demonstrate that the process is broken, or doesn't work the way it should, or is hard to use. Allow the customers to provide context if they want, but if they don't, you receive all the information you need to make a fix.

Of course, all the investment in feedback mechanisms will be a waste if banks don't spend time fixing the problems. Having an analytic approach to prioritize problems by customer value, potential disruption, and revenue impact will help build a business case to making it work correctly. Just make sure if your bank asks, it reacts.

Problems don't just exist in banking technology; often they exist in banking practices. Some of those practices are not only easily fixable with data and analytics, they represent violations of existing laws and regulations.

One area that tends to not get fixed is in the data handling around credit and collections. Often, banks do not spend a lot of money getting this experience right because these are not profitable customers. But the compliance costs of getting it wrong can be astronomical.

A recent report[21] from the Consumer Financial Protection Bureau (CFPB), the main consumer protection agency for US banking customer, stated that credit bureaus, debt collectors, and payday lenders are often not fulfilling their obligations under the law to transfer documentation of debt accurately and follow up on consumer disputes. Add to that the continued abusive practices of some debt collectors in violation of US Federal laws, and you have a real customer problem.

Given that consumers today are more empowered to fight back against incorrect credit reporting and debt collection activities, banks would be wise to get this part of their operations in order. It's just a matter of time before regulators trace back these bad actions to the sellers of the original debts.

Make It Understandable

You can't talk about banking in the press these days without mentioning the word transparency. After decades without it, transparency is all the rage among customer and regulators alike. And it's not a pretty picture for this industry.

In a recent survey[22] of global banking consumers, EY asked about the importance and satisfaction levels for different attributes. A serious warning sign would be any attribute that was of above average importance and below average satisfaction. The biggest

[21] "Supervisory Highlights," Consumer Financial Protection Bureau, Spring 2014.
[22] Global Consumer Banking Survey 2014: "Winning through customer experience," Report, EY

outlier—being in the top half on importance and bottom half on satisfaction—was the statement: "[My bank] is transparent about what they charge for and makes it clear to you how to avoid paying fees."

Gulp.

Customers are saying they don't even know what they're paying for and how much. In addition, they're telling banks they want to avoid paying for things, but they can't figure out how!

That is an indictment.

How can customers trust the real-time alerts and data they so desperately crave if they can't even trust their bank's pricing? This must be fixed.

You may be wondering how to create pricing transparency when I just had a whole chapter dedicated to individual pricing technologies. Transparency is not uniformity. And by the way, that's a note to regulators too. Transparency is about communicating with customers on price in a way they understand.

When banks can let their customers know how their financial product will affect their customer's budget in a real way, they're transparent. Customers don't react well to hedges and risk shifting. That's why so many adjustable-rate mortgages with provisions in the case of dropping home equity were horrible. No one could figure out the impact of those loans; not the broker and in some cases, not the servicer. So how in the world did banks expect their customers to figure it out?

Sure, there is a market for advanced, sophisticated hedging products. They're called investors. These kinds of products have no room in the retail bank. They're fundamentally lazy, shifting uncalculated risk to unsuspecting party.

It's that fundamental lack of parity in the transaction that customers sense. They feel like banks know something they don't, and they don't like it. So in turn, they've nailed their banks for it. Rightly so.

Make It Fast
There is still a lot of work to do in creating more efficient customer experiences.

Nicole Sturgill, a research director at CEB TowerGroup, explains the task in front of us,

> Let's look [for example] at how the customer has resolved an issue. What were the steps they had to take? How many people did they have to talk to [in order] to get that issue resolved? And if we could take all of that out, what would the process look like? Start there. Do that for all of your processes and then you have an improved customer experience.[23]

Process re-engineering is not a new concept. There have been some great examples in banking lately of taking processes and re-thinking them from scratch.

Hana Bank in South Korea took the process of getting a mortgage and re-engineered it. The result is the One Click Mortgage. The product has five steps: e-application, e-underwriting, e-signing, e-document, and e-closing. Borrowers do not need to visit any branches or have face-to-face meetings. The entire process is online. A mortgage is usually the worst and most difficult financial

---

[23] "Interview with Nicole Sturgill, Research Director, Retail Banking CEB TowerGroup," YouTube, February 7, 2014.

product, and Hana Bank has made it faster and easier for everyone.

Turkish Economy Bank (TEB) in Turkey made the process at the ATM faster with QR-codes. The service allows customers to withdraw funds from the ATM with a QR code. That code creates a unique, customer-specific mobile PIN. From there, it's one step at the ATM to get money. Not only is the process faster and simpler, by integrating multi-factor authentication, it's safer too.

Context and data can go a long way to make processes faster. Many of the stages in a process are information gathering. In many of those cases, the bank already possesses the data it's requesting; it just doesn't know it yet. Smart devices, context, and single sign-on can help move these stages along.

Silos also create problems. In one large bank in the United States, you can apply for a boat loan over the phone. The customer still needs to sign paper documents, which already is a bad customer experience. But to make matters worse, although the bank has an extensive branch network, the borrower cannot simply sign the documents at a branch. They need to be sent via overnight mail, signed, and resent in order to close the loan. The excuse is that the boat loan folks don't talk to the branch folks. That's a silly excuse, and banks shouldn't be surprised when their customers don't accept it.

Anticipate the appropriate time to response. One critical mistake banks still make today is not aligning their back-office operation availability with their front office. The most serious example is in fraud detection. Most banks today have a 24/7 response to credit card fraud. If a card is used somewhere in the world that the bank thinks is suspicious, it will act immediately to freeze the card and stop any potential criminal activity.

150

When the customer finds this out, many banks do not have a 24/7 customer center ready to help with the fallout. If a customer has to wait until the next business day to fix the problem and get his card turned back on, the fault is squarely with the bank. The bank chose to take action in real-time and provided no real-time way for the customer to reverse its action.

What makes this example so horrible is that the banks *know* there is a chance they're wrong. They do it anyways, inconveniencing their customers and providing no relief until it's convenient for them. There's no excuse for this kind of customer experience.

When customers today are used to "one-click" buying buttons on websites and same-day delivery, banks are competing on a very different playing field than they were before. There is no more time to allow customers to struggle with slow processes that repeat steps, ask for duplicate information, and don't anticipate needs.

Transform It to a Value-Add

Most bank processes are a "must do." Customers know that there are things they have to do to comply with bank policy or government regulation.

But imagine how much different the experience would be if the bank could change a "must do" into a "want to." The key is finding a customer value-add.

I don't mean a fake value-add. Often banks give excuses to their customers. Things they make them do "for their own safety." In the example we just discussed, banks restrict the usage of a credit card while a customer is traveling, usually at the worst possible time, and when the customer calls to complain about how awful the experience was, it was all "for their safety."

It's not. Fraudulent transactions are not the customer's responsibility assuming they report them in time. This is all about keeping the bank safe. And the customers know it.

So, let's talk about real value-adds.

There isn't a high bar for what constitutes a value-add, by the way. Many companies in other industries have made huge improvements in the engagement level of customers by using gamification, the use of certain game elements in an online activity. Those game elements can include things like point scoring, prizes, competition with other "players", or rules.

When Bell Media's MuchMusic website rewarded return users with champion status, they saw a 33% increase in daily retention, a 21% increase in registered users, and a 59% lift in overall behaviors as a result. Gaining badges or profile points isn't a monetary value, but for some customers, especially in the newer digital generations, it's enough. And given that gamification rewards are free, the value proposition is easy.

And research backs that up. A recent survey[24] by the Aberdeen Group showed that organizations with gamification increase engagement level by 48% compared with 28% for those that don't. Additionally, those organizations improve turnover by 36% compared to 25% of those who do not employ gamification.

Banks shouldn't dismiss gamification as not applicable in the banking sector. A 2013 survey[25] of global banks showed that 45% of banks have already invested in or plan to invest in gamification technology to attract customers.

---

[24] "Sales Effectiveness 2013: The Rise of #Gamification", Report, Aberdeen Group. February 2013.
[25] "Innovation in Retail Banking 2013," Survey, Infosys and EFMA, October 2013.

But beyond the virtual currency, there is plenty of opportunity in the real thing. Many banks are starting to add in identity protection in their underwriting process. When a bank opens a deposit account in the United States, it checks a central database for accounts that other banks may have closed because of fraud or other unreimbursed losses.

That process can be very painful especially if the customer is a victim of identity theft. But many banks now refer certain customer segments to a bank representative in the case of decline. Those representatives contact the customer directly to confirm the application did in fact origination with them. They also can notify the customer of the negative reports and put them in touch with the appropriate resources to help clear up the problem or notate their records appropriately. That's a very different experience than simply receiving an adverse action letter in the mail.

Banks need to review their processes and find ways they can add value to the customer instead of simply having them trudge through each step. Satisfaction and engagement levels will go up. The process will transform from a "must do" to a delight.

HELPING CUSTOMERS MAKE BETTER DECISIONS

Let's break down the decisions customers need to make on a day-to-day basis. The "moments that matter" in the customer's financial life include the following:

- Making money
- Borrowing money
- Paying people
- Saving money
- Spending money

Making Money

Unless your bank has a way of helping people get a better job (hey, not a bad idea—just credit me with it), it helps its customers make more money mainly through investment advice. That could mean formal investment planning but it could be as simple as picking a checking account that earns interest.

Bankers spend most of their advice-giving time in this area. It's the area, which, for the vast majority of customers, has the least short-term impact. Obviously, as investment advisors, bankers argue that the long-term impact is what customers should be thinking about. Maslow's hierarchy of needs should tell you they're wrong.

If you're not familiar with Maslow, his theory is that you can't get people focused on higher-level needs when they don't have food, clothing, and shelter. Usually that's a metaphor, but in this case, it may actually be the point.

The majority of customers need help in managing their budgets and housing payments. If they can't do that, how in the world can banks get them focused on saving for retirement? This industry has ignored this gap long enough. (But we'll get to that in a moment.)

Banks are good at identifying those customers who are looking to drive income from their banking and investment activities. I won't spend any more time on that, but keep in mind that there are a lot of items around income generation for customers that banks don't serve today. In helping customers make money, for a vast majority of them, banks are playing around the margin.

Borrowing Money

One half of most banks is dedicated to this one decision customers make: how and when to borrow money. The fundamental business challenge here is that this is a decision most customers don't want to make.

That friction is summed up well by Ron Shevlin, senior analyst at Aite Group:

> Borrowing money... is just one part of the money management problem. Consumers don't **want** to borrow money, they **need** to. Mark my words: You will always make more money by providing what consumers want than what they need. Sure, they'll pay for what they need, but will look to minimize that expense. Serving their desires, on the other hand...[emphasis included in original][26]

Add to that friction the fact that many customers (and regulators) now distrust the banking industry to fairly provide this service, and the industry has a serious problem.

The growth of alternative sources of funds such as peer-to-peer lending is an outlet for that frustration. If consumers are going to pay, they're going to pay the lowest amount possible. Industry after industry, the most common way of reducing cost is reducing the middleman; yes, banks are the middleman.

You may argue that banks a value-added middleman by managing risk, but they're a middleman nonetheless.

What that means is that the product they're offering is risk management. Many banks fear that if they turn their default and prepayment models outward to the public with the money that they will lose their business.

---

[26] "Banking Myopia", Ron Shevlin, Snarketing 2.0 by Ron Shevlin Blog, March 17, 2014

I'm here to tell you that the business is lost. Not that no one will ever borrow from a bank again, but the concept that the bank is a required intermediary between the (true) lender and the borrower is now provably false. It no longer has a future as a middleman.

So what is the *unmet* need here: it's access to money with less hassle and at lower expense. If you believe Ron Shevlin, borrowing money is a commodity, not a value-added service. Turn it into a value-added service and you've got something.

But when something becomes a commodity, it's a tough place to make a living. Commodities still need support. The value-added service may lie in the support of the commodity trading. Be the platform. Supply the emerging market. Help customers find the sources. And embrace the change.

Like all verticals, elimination of the middleman comes with bumps and bruises. There will be some spectacular failures along the way. But there will be enough successes. Every time this is tried, the middleman always goes away eventually.

You might argue that the same is true on the savings side, so why bother? Well, you're right. High-end investment tools have made it easier to invest without a broker. Ask brokers if they don't feel like middlemen sometimes. But the decision where to invest your money is significantly more complex.

Consider all the variables necessary to decide where to invest your money versus where to borrow your money from. It's a lot easier to decide from whom to borrow. Tools will continue to emerge making the investment and savings decision easier, but the ease of decision is not keeping people from cutting out the middleman in borrowing. It's a platform. And those exist already with Prosper and LendingClub. More will come.

Banks that will succeed in the end will make this process easier and cheaper. Banks that continue to put up roadblocks or act as gatekeepers for funds will lose.

Paying People

The growth of the payments industry proves the importance of having an efficient method of paying people. The industry has responded via peer-to-peer (P2P) payments and bill payment. Both are gaining steam.

Many banks have chosen to sit on the sidelines and wait out the P2P payment game. This is a mistake for two reasons. First, by sitting around waiting to see who will emerge the victor, banks are guaranteed *not* to be the victor. Second, the victor will not share the spoils.

What are the spoils of payments? The data.

Andy Schmidt, a research director for CEB TowerGroup, said the following:

> *Banks that embrace the future and invest in the new payments technologies will end up with a competitive advantage— namely, an enormous wealth of data about their customers' spending habits. This data will soon open a floodgate of new bank products tailored to customer needs, generating new revenue streams and bolstering customer retention.*[27]

Many analysts who have looked at the payments space have mistakenly written it off as transaction processing technology. While those are table stakes, the benefit far exceeds the

---

[27] "Payment Due", Andy Schmidt, ABA Bank Marketing, November 2013.

commodity movement of the money. Much like Google, it doesn't build its business plan on the connection between the searcher and website; it's all about the data.

But the need is clear. In a recent survey,[28] 13.2% of smartphone users made a mobile P2P payment within the last 30 days. That's up 30% from the previous survey 9 months prior.

The problem is that the same survey showed the proportion of customers using bank or credit union apps to do this declined. Banks are losing the race.

Saving Money

When I talk about saving money, I want to be clear that I'm referring to putting money away for a future goal. Saving money can also mean spending less, but we'll cover that next.

I also don't want to focus on investment or savings for retirement. Banks clearly have a lot of work to do improving how they help people save for retirement. There are plenty of books, however, on that topic and I think it's one well understood in the industry.

But going back to Maslow for a moment, what about saving for things before retirement? Even among investment advisors, there are two major objectives: retirement (long-term) and short-term. The overwhelming volume of content is written on long-term investing.

Yet most customers have a short-term problem. It shows up as credit card debt and payday lending. They can't manage their short-term cash needs. And if you're making monthly payments on a credit card or revolving bi-weekly payday loans, you're certainly not thinking about your income needs at age 65.

---

[28] FindABetterBank.com customer survey, January 2014

We used to encourage savings for short-term goals. Remember the Christmas club account? It gained its height of popularity in the 1970s in the United States. For those not familiar, a Christmas club was a short-term savings vehicle to help put money away for Christmas. You could open them with very little money, and you couldn't touch the money until closer to your goal date. They still exist, mostly at small banks and credit unions, but their popularity is way down.

The industry mostly killed them off. Minimum balances, low to no interest rate, and monthly maintenance fees make short-term savings accounts an economic impossibility. But make no mistake, the need is still there. A recent report by the Consumer Federation of America (CFA) showed that "these basic savings accounts represent the best source of funds for [low and moderate income families], and even many middle-income, families to pay for unexpected expenses such as car repairs and many medical and dental bills."[29]

Banks can make a business from small spending goals that encourage savings and incentivize the saver to not touch the money. It's a matter of technology and focus. It could be in the short-term that the account itself does nothing more than anchor the customer to the bank. Calculate that value and include it in your profit and loss statement.

Spending Money

Arguably, spending money is the task that consumers do most often. It's also the task around which banks spend the least amount of time advising. If anything, the industry has a conflicting message on spending: spend more, but we'll ding you if it's too

---

[29] "Savings Accounts: Their Characteristics and Usefulness," Stephen Brobeck, Consumer Federation of America, June 2013.

much. But how much is too much? Basically, bankers offer no other suggestions.

There are two fundamental customer needs that must be addressed:

1. How much money can I spend?
2. How do I spend less?

Some would argue that personal financial management (PFM) tools are built to handle the first point. I would not be one of them. PFM tools built around categorization and budgeting have very low adoption rates, as we've already discussed. That's because they still, fundamentally, don't help answer the question: how much should/can I spend?

PFM tools have been built mostly to help people get a sense of their financial picture. But in this case, a picture doesn't paint enough words. Remember, the issue here is decision-making in a complex environment. If you think most consumers can figure the answer to that question out from some graphs and charts, you're sorely mistaken.

Customers need much more direct recommendations. Some vendors are starting this. The new startup bank, Simple, provides more of this guidance as part of their PFM tools. They provide a "safe to spend" number based on the account balance, pending transactions, and committed bills.

That's a great start, but it doesn't answer the whole question. There are other factors that are a part of the problem. Future scheduled deposits, unusually large transactions, and expected outflows that haven't been manually scheduled all come together to make this problem more complicated. But customers say they want it solved.

160

Let's turn our attention to the second issue: spending less money.

Several banks have rolled out discounts to their customers. Those discounts focus on merchants the bank has a relationship with, and they encourage spending in categories that matter to the individual customer. There are definitely beneficial economics for helping customers save money when it drives purchases to particular merchants. But beyond that, customers have indicated that this is important to them.

And if it's important to customers, it should be important to banks. In a recent survey[30] of banking customers, 82% indicated that they are extremely interested in having their bank save them money. And 72% feel that saving money would increase their loyalty to the bank.

Experiments are going on in Asia related to geo-location specific offers. This was the same scenario we described back in the last section on next best offer. Early feedback from the market focuses on two main findings:

1. Customers do, in fact, appreciate discounts in spending from their bank.
2. Offers that are not relevant are a nuisance and viewed negatively; offers that are relevant, however, are a value-add and viewed positively—this is a double-edge sword.
3. The strength of the analytics is a key success factor.

Most banks have shied away from offering merchant-specific discounts because they feel like it's spamming in a way. But, what we've learned across industries is that there is a fine-line between spam and value-add; it's all about the analytics.

---

[30] "The Digital Disruption in Banking: Demons, demands, and dividends," 2014 North America Consumer Digital Banking Survey, Accenture, 2014.

Another reason banks shy away from this kind of offering is because it "doesn't feel like banking." I reject that excuse. Banking is what creates long-term value for the customers. And the data shows, many customers want discounts.

BECOMING AN ADVOCATE WHEN THINGS GO WRONG

There are two major ways something could go wrong in the financial life of the customer. Usually when bankers think of customer problems, they think of things going wrong with the bank. In addition to that, however, sometimes things just go wrong.

If the bank wants to become an advocate for the financial life of the customer, bankers need to handle both.

When Things Go Wrong at the Bank

As part of EY's global consumer banking survey, they identified two attributes that customers listed as above average importance when dealing with their bank:

1. Works with you when you need help or encounter a problem.
2. Reaches out if problem may exist.

The first item was lower in importance than the second, but it was also more highly rated in satisfaction. Note that proactive, "push" alerts are very important to customers.

First, let me make an argument for the fact that this is an unmet need. Carlisle & Gallagher released a report[31] on customer complaint management. It showed that, according to survey respondents, only 62% of problems were completely resolved,

---

[31] "Are Two Calls Too Many in the Eyes of the Customer?" White Paper, Carlisle & Gallagher, December 2013.

and 20% of problems weren't resolved at all. In addition, the same survey showed that of the problems that were resolved, 72% of them required two or more interactions to reach a resolution.

But does that matter? Those same respondents indicated that 22% of the customers who had their problem resolved in one call said they provided more business to their bank. Compare that to 10% of those customers where it took more than 2 or more interactions to solve the problem.

On the flip side, 63% of customers whose problem went unresolved said they did less business or even ended their relationship with the bank. Compare that to just 4% of those customers whose problem was resolved in one interaction.

So, it's a problem and it's worth solving. Let's move on.

Empower employees to fix the problem the first time. Monitor to ensure compliance and that the bank is being protected, but stop imposing multi-layered approval levels to fix things you know are going wrong already. If your bank allows fees to be waived, put an analytic-based fee waiver decision-making system in place so it isn't leaving it up to the front-line to decide. Don't put people on hold and transfer to a manager.

If I can search practically every book every published online in a few seconds, you do not need several business days to research transactions on your customers' accounts. There is no good excuse here except staffing; resolve the problem.

Disputing charges should be much easier. Especially because recent research shows that banks and merchant processors are complicit in some of the "grey charges" ending up on people cards. Gray charges aren't exactly illegal or fraudulent, but they are not the result of a fully informed business transaction. They occur because of either a change in the business terms or an unknown business term.

Aite Group published a report[32] on these grey charges and found that more than 40% of those charges came from "free-to-premium" services. The ones that start out free, but you have to give a credit card to sign up. Often, the company begins charging your card without warning.

Worse than that, there is a bit of a conflict of interest involved. The author of the report, Ron Shevlin, concludes[33]:

> Though grey charges aren't technically fraudulent, they present a dilemma for credit and debit card issuers: generate interchange fees from grey charges or incur service-related expenses when cardholders dispute charges.

Too often, customers are victims to businesses who sign people up for contract payments and then make cancellation nearly impossible. Banks who are interested in providing services to their customers will step in. In fact, the UK recently mandated that banks and mutuals will be required to cancel a recurring payment upon request of the customer without requiring them to go back to the merchant. It would be great if the United States did the same.

I'm not arguing for banks to protect people from themselves. If the merchant putting through the recurring payments provided an easy way to cancel, there would be no problem. But if banks are making money off of these interchange fees and their client—the bad-acting merchants—are playing dirty, the banks should be required to step in.

---

[32] "The Economic Impact of Grey Charges on Debit and Credit Card Issuers," Ron Shevlin, Aite Group, Report, July 2013.
[33] Ibid.

When Things Go Wrong in Life

Life is messy. Lots of things can go wrong. I want to focus on two big ones.

1. The customer suddenly can't pay his bills.
2. The customer has been the victim of some kind of fraud or theft.

Today, when consumers realize they have a cash flow problem, the last person they want to talk to is their bank. That's a shame; the bank is probably best equipped to help the customer through the problem. Beyond providing automated tools that could show the customers where they can cut spending, the bank could immediately notify all creditors (not just the ones at the bank) and provide short-term cash flow sources, even if not at the bank.

Imagine if your bank were that kind of advocate. It would drastically change your relationship with the customer, and the head's up you would get on potential defaults would be invaluable. Why do customers have to turn to some sleazy companies to get debt management help?

There is a huge need to provide debt and spending management services to customers who find themselves in trouble, whether of their own fault or not. Banks that can capitalize on that need and provide value-added services and not simply react by punishing the customers for their "bad actions" will be wildly successful. There is money in fixing that problem.

Sometimes the bad thing that happens is no fault of the customer; he is the victim of some kind of theft or fraud. That can range from having a credit card stolen, to being charged for something he didn't buy, to having his entire identity stolen.

I want to point out a pet peeve of mine. Banks need to stop signing people up for credit monitoring when their credit card numbers have been stolen and then declaring victory. In response to a recent major security breach at the retailer Target, Mick Weinstein, the CMO at Billguard said[34]:

> This [signing people up for credit monitoring services] is a well-intended effort... but anyone who's familiar with card fraud understands that it won't actually help anyone right away. Credit monitoring services don't function on the transaction level, so if someone actually uses your credit card in the period soon after it's stolen, the credit reporting agencies simply won't notice it.

Similar to debt and spending management, there is value in the bank providing relief to those affected by fraud and theft. That service goes beyond simply removing the charges. It's not a "service" to avoid charging people for things they didn't buy.

Banks often claim that the security protocols of their merchants are not their problem. I disagree. Before banks sign up large merchants, they should audit and be accountable for their security procedures. After all, the bank profits when the merchant transacts. It's not like it's a charity.

The bank that steps out to provide a value-added service, enhanced by the transaction data and analytics they have access to, will step into a much-needed hole where customers are currently suffering.

Unmet Customer Needs Recap:
I focused on three major areas where customer needs are often unmet:

---

[34] "Are credit cards hopelessly insecure?" Mick Weinstein, Medium.com, January 2014.

1. Clear and simple banking
2. Helping customer make decisions in a complex environment
3. Advocating for the customer when things go wrong

Clear and simple banking comes in four stages:

1. Fix the problems.
2. Make it understandable.
3. Make it fast.
4. Transform it to a value-add.

The major decisions customers need to make in this ever-increasingly complex financial world are:

- Making money
- Borrowing money
- Paying people
- Saving money
- Spending money

And finally, advocacy should be focused on when things go wrong at the bank as well as when things go wrong in the customer's life.

CHAPTER 12. CREATING FINANCIAL PRODUCTS OF THE FUTURE

When the industry discusses innovation in banking products, it often gets sidetracked into discussions about better ways of communicating with customers, such as channel improvements, or better features and functionality so that customers can get more relevant information about the state of their financial affairs.

But that's not enough. Banks need to actually create new financial products that don't exist today. These products don't just make communication and information sharing easier; they meet unmet needs. The vast majority of the innovations in banking improve access to information— making a process easier, rather than creating something that doesn't exist.

The good news is that innovative in banking is happening. A 2013 survey of budgets in 148 banks in 66 countries revealed that 77% of banks have increased spending on innovation, compared with 13% in 2009.[35]

This chapter is going to dive into the frontiers of banking— meeting needs that banks don't even think about today. And I'll relate back to the needs I surfaced in the last chapter.

I want to spend some time telling some cool stories about new innovation as well as provide some insight into how to (and how

---

[35] "Innovation in Retail Banking," Survey, Infosys and European Financial Marketing Association (EFMA), October 2013.

not to) roll out new products and features. Hopefully, the creativity of banking staffs can capitalize on the needs and the success stories to create their own.

NOT INVENTED HERE (IN THE WESTERN HEMISPHERE)

One of the most striking things about banking innovation is the vast majority of it is happening in Asia right now. That has been the case from at least 2010–2014.

It's a bit unfortunate. The United States and parts of Western Europe have been at the forefront of analytic development. The vast majority of risk management techniques were first used in the United States: risk-based pricing, credit scoring, and secure lending. These innovations were exported throughout the rest of the world. In most banks in emerging markets in which I've personally consulted, they always ask me what is happening in the United States. Since 2012, they also ask, "How can we avoid their mistakes?"

That's a great question. You could write a whole book on the credit crisis mistakes of 2008–2012, but that's not our focus here. I will, however, point out a critical mistake that's happening today. Regulation is the number one killer of innovation.

The irony is that I'm not arguing against all banking regulation, but it is clear that the Western Hemisphere is losing the innovation race to Asia because they are under the gun of government regulators. It's more than just budgets being diverted. It's a culture of "don't dare fail." That culture is the sign of a company not willing to innovate. And it shows.

Regulation isn't going away, and banks have to deal with it somehow. I'll address this issue specifically in a later chapter. But for now, let's at least acknowledge what it is doing to innovation in the industrialized banking world.

MEETING THOSE UNMET NEEDS

I want to provide a few examples from each of the unmet needs we discussed in the previous chapter. I'll talk about the banks or vendors that have implemented those solutions and why they are so innovative.

Your bank may not want to implement the same thing, or even something similar. But hopefully the creativity of meeting some of these customers' needs triggers ideas about how your bank can accelerate the evolution of the industry.

Clear and Simple Banking

One common challenge among young adults is the transition to financial independence. Often, when high school and new college students are starting out, their financial lives are a blend of their own and their parents. Banks don't make it easy to span that gap, as account titling is either joint or separate—there's nothing half way.

But teens and students often have to make financial decisions and then ask their parents to back them up either completely or partially. The industry makes steps in this direction by offering co-signing on loans, but for spending, it's less collaborative.

A new service, BillMyParents, offers a prepaid debit card that is loaded up by the parent and used by the child. Unlike independent accounts, this service allows parents information about spending via text message. If the parent feels like the child is being irresponsible, they can lock the card with a quick SMS.

In case of emergencies, parents can load money onto the card from anywhere so their children can access it. The funds are available instantly. And since the parents can monitor transactions and balances, they are in complete control.

What's fundamentally innovative about this solution is the emerging prominence of prepaid debit cards. A popular product among the "underbanked," prepaid debit cards offer the flexibility of plastic—as seems to be required in our world— without tying themselves to a traditional checking account with all the risks of overdrafts and overhead.

Prepaid debit cards and their descendants, pre-loaded P2P payments, will become a central feature of banking. It won't be the right solution for everyone, but they are like the MP3 singles that replaced the album-only sales of the last few decades. They represent choice in banking a la carte.

Bulgarian bank Borica has recently rolled out a new service called CashM. It allows customers to send money to other people who can pick up their money at an ATM. This fundamentally reduces a step in the money-transfer process. No longer do customers need to come into a money center and collect the cash. They can retrieve it as easily as they would any other withdrawal.

The sender initiates a transfer from his own bank account either at an ATM or in branch. The mobile number of the recipient is the key identifier for the transaction, including a four-digit code generated by the service. The sender provides the code to the recipient. Once approved, the service sends an SMS to the recipient along with another six-digit code. These codes, along with their mobile number, are the authentication parameters used at the ATM. The service is intended for low-dollar personal transfers and is limited to around $275 USD.

What's truly innovative about this service is the removal of steps from a cumbersome process of getting cash. This is an important missing piece even among many P2P payments players. Unless the recipient has an account or other relationship with the payment provider, getting cash to people far away can be difficult and involves lengthy ACH transfers or other cumbersome methods.

That requirement has been a challenge in getting very fast growth in some P2P payment technologies: the recipient, not just the sender, needs to belong. In this service, the recipient doesn't need an account with Borica Bankservice; he simply puts his codes into the ATM.

Helping Customers Make Decisions

We've discussed the upstart bank, Simple, recently acquired by BBVA. Their mobile application includes a new feature called Safe-to-Spend which shows the customer not just his current balance, but his balance after scheduled transaction and savings goals.

This is a step closer to the cash-flow management tools customers need. Add advanced analytics and forecasting and the true power of using analytics to benefit the customer becomes evident. It's like a bank takes their own internal analytics capabilities and "turns it outward" to help the customer.

What makes this so innovative is the breakout of the traditional "balance-centric" view of banking. With debit card transactions waiting to be cleared and the odd outstanding check, current and available balances are essentially useless for consumers. The digital generation doesn't even know what it means to balance a checkbook. They need financial metrics for today, and this is a step in the right direction.

Another new service, ReadyForZero, is intended to help consumers make better decisions about borrowing and getting out of debt faster. The individualized plan it creates shows the impact of payments, sets goals, and projects a timeline to be debt free. It even offers credit-score monitoring to sync with the payoff plan.

The service is mobile and sends push alerts based on activity on the monitored debt accounts. Scheduled and targeted alerts keep consumers on track and will even set up recurring payments from their accounts so they can pay off their debt without even thinking about it.

The graphical user interface gives consumers a way to see the financial impact of their goals and the progress they've made along the way. It's a perfect example of targeted PFM, focused on the single decision of getting out of debt.

What makes this so innovative is the laser-focused goal of the product. It takes on one issue, one pain point, and tackles it for the consumer. Since financial management is simply a set of decisions, this is a perfect way of undertake one of the most difficult for people.

Becoming an Advocate for the Customer
Unfortunately, this is one area where few banks and vendors have come forward with solutions. Aside from standard debt consolidation and management plans to create a new payment plan, there isn't much innovation for customers who run into cash-flow challenges.

One vendor that has stood out in the identity protection crowd is LifeLock. While many vendors are describing monitoring services, LifeLock goes one step beyond. Their mobile application has a

"Not Me" feature that allows you to respond to potential identity threats in real-time.

Members can even count on LifeLock to actively fight any repercussions of identity theft by assigning a resolution specialist to the case.

In fact, they promise to spend up to $1 million to hire experts to help members recover. That staff could include lawyers, investigators, and consultants. Where most services only include notifications and "fraud alerts" on your credit report, LifeLock actually fights back— advocates—for their members.

AGILE BANKING

Perhaps you've heard of agile software development. It's a new technique often described as incremental or iterative based on the idea that you cannot possibly scope out everything you might want in a software product at the beginning. It requires the integration of user stories and quick iteration cycles to "get it right."

Banking needs to be the same way. Many of the IT projects are large, enterprise-wide endeavors. But when it comes to rolling out innovation, the industry needs to use agile banking.

Let's start off by looking at the agile principles and map it to our own. There are 12 principles of agile development. (I recommend the Agile Manifesto[36] if you're interested in reading them.) I want to modify them to create the 12 principles of *agile banking*.

1. Satisfy the Customer Early and Often
The only thing that matters is customer profitability. It's no longer a debate that customer satisfaction and loyalty bring revenue.

---

[36] http://AgileManifesto.org/principles.html

With so many alternative players itching to get into the market, there is no time for delay.

2. Welcome Changing Customer Needs
They say the only thing constant is change. It's true with customers as well. The expectation level of the consumer increases every day. New products and devices appear all the time, and they are raising the bar. It is a never-ending battle to meet those changing needs.

3. Deliver Value-Add Frequently
Banks can improve service levels and iron out the bugs in their current processes. To truly become the personalized bank of the future and innovate, banks have to deliver value. That means new not just improved.

4. Innovate with Customers
Often we dream up new ideas in a vacuum and only afterwards test them with customers. One bank in the south-eastern United States reported that only after engaging customers in real-life testing of new products would they see good adoption. Involve customers early and often.

5. Build Innovation Teams
Banks must staff for innovation. Find motivated, engaged employees who are dedicated to customer satisfaction and dare to challenge the status quo. There is no room for naysayers and yes-men.

6. Gather Feedback Face-to-Face
If a bank does not have a forum to meet with customers face-to-face to receive feedback, it must correct that error now. It's not good enough to solicit the occasional comment via surveys. It needs to have a board of customers who constantly challenge the bank to bigger and better things. Meet with them face-to-face.

7. Define Success as Value Creation

If your bank is still struggling with the complexities of customer lifetime value, substitute meeting customer needs. It will be a good proxy until it dials in the numbers. In the short-term, it may be a losing proposition. But the long-term play is worth it.

8. Maintain a Constant Pace Indefinitely

Innovation is not a program; it's a lifestyle. Start with a plan to never stop. Short bursts of new features will simply tell customers not to expect anything from your bank. Get them to expect constant progress.

9. Give Continuous Attention to Customer Excellence

Don't allow the numbers to drive bad customer decisions. Typically these short-sighted calculations are incomplete. When banks do the real math— the long-term math— satisfying the customers' needs always comes out profitable.

10. Simplify: Focus on What Matters Most

It's easy to get distracted by the latest technology fad. Just find out what the customer wants and provide it. There is a concept in agile development called the minimum viable product (MVP). Find a single focus and deliver to it.

11. Don't Wait to Be Told What's Wrong

Be proactive. Don't fix it when it's broken. Fix it before it breaks. Your bank generally knows what needs work. Don't wait until a customer has to point it out.

12. Question Everything; Then Change

The day of the sacred cow is over. There's no more time left for the industry to say "it's always been this way." Those days are over. No more excuses; none are good enough: not legacy systems, not compliance, not regulators, not internal skill set. If your banks don't question it, someone else will.

Innovative Financial Products Recap:
If not properly monitored, government regulation could be the number one barrier to creating the robust and dynamic banking environment necessary to sustain growth and innovation. The banking industry needs to lobby regulators to strike an appropriate balance between risk management and allowing creation of innovative financial products.

Banks will excel in creating those financial products by focusing on the unmet needs of their customers. I outlined three major categories:

1. Clear and simple banking
2. Helping customers make decisions in a complex environment
3. Advocating for the customer when things go wrong

Taking a page from the software industry that is undergoing its own transformation into more innovative and responsive companies, banking can be more agile. I outlined banking's own agile manifesto with twelve guiding principles:

1. Satisfy the customer early and often
2. Welcome changing customer needs
3. Delivery value-add frequently
4. Innovate with customers
5. Build innovation teams
6. Gather feedback face-to-face
7. Define success as value creation
8. Maintain a constant pace indefinitely
9. Give continuous attention to customer excellence
10. Simplify: focus on what matters most

11. Don't wit to be told what's wrong
12. Question everything; then change

PART V: HOW CAN BANKS GET THERE?

It doesn't do a lot of good talking about change if the banking industry can't find the path. Otherwise, it's like standing at a trailhead looking up at a mountain peak wondering how nice the view is from up there. If there's no map or trail, it's just a fantasy.

This section should act as the roadmap. I obviously cannot give turn-by-turn directions, but there are systems and processes that will be impacted. Since leveraging analytics for a personalized banking experience is the goal, I would hope analytics would provide some help along the way.

Banks can't make wholesale changes to their business and how they interact with clients without thinking about the regulatory impact of those changes. I'll discuss those changes and how a personalized banking experience that maximizes the long-term value of the customer is in harmony with broad regulatory goals.

This section will answer the questions:

1.   What systems and processes will need to change in the bank to make this happen?
2.   How will regulators likely react to these changes and will they approve?
3.   What does the step-by-step map look like for a bank making these changes?

Chapter 13. Regulatory and Compliance Impact

If you look at government regulation and the compliance programs, you know they exist to prevent three fundamental things from happening.

First, they intend to prevent the bank from taking advantage of the customer in an unfair way. Second, they intend to prevent "bad things" from happening like fraud and financial crimes. And finally, they intend to prevent the bank from failing and having to be bailed out by the government.

I hate to cast things in such a negative light, but this is government regulation I'm talking about here. It may be a necessary evil, but an evil it is nonetheless.

While avoiding these three things is good, rules and regulations are often crafted in a way that has far-reaching, unintended consequences. Regulation is the number one killer of innovation in banking, as I've already mentioned. In order to transform into the industry bankers know they can become, they'll have to do it in spite of government rules built—in some ways— to prevent that very thing from happening.

Let's talk about each of these three purposes and discuss how to achieve the three pillars of mobile banking, next best action, and innovative financial products in concert with governmental oversight.

Not Taking Advantage of Customers

Of course one of the big things regulators are concerned about is when banks do things that take advantage of their customers. It doesn't have to be something malicious to take advantage of customers, banks can simply enter a new transaction that the customers don't understand, don't need, or don't want.

As mentioned earlier, customers are telling banks that they have a difficult time understanding pricing and how to avoid paying for things that they don't think is a value-add. And so there are three things that a personalized individual banking experience can do to avoid taking advantage of the customer that will also keep regulators at bay.

1. A personalized bank doesn't hide things from its customers. Because the banks have done the data analysis to create an individualized experience and product offers that maximize the customer's lifetime value, it doesn't need to hide the fact that the product offer is not a good fit. The bank avoids all of the issues around mis-selling[37] or bad product fit because it designed a product offer in a particular way. If the bank finds that the product offered to the customers is problematic or causes issues for them, then it hasn't done its work correctly; the math doesn't add up.

And so the banks are able to be completely forthright and honest because they are building a value proposition that they can buy in to. The vast majority of problems that banks face around mis-selling have to do with incentivized sales teams that are pushing a particular product and of course, they're under pressure to push enough of that volume that they push the product even to those

---

[37] Mis-selling is a British term for selling the wrong product to the wrong customer, often with a nefarious intent or negligent attitude about the value for the customer

people who aren't a good fit for it. But when they're offering an individualized banking experience to everyone, the volume they need to generate is the sum total of all of the different products. They don't have to create a volume of scale artificially based on a product that may not have a marketplace for itself.

2. Transparency is not uniformity, but is a value-add. We discussed this issue earlier when we talked about the fact that being transparent with customers does not mean offering the same thing to everyone. This is something that still confuses regulators today. They view uniformity as a substitution for transparency, primarily because they don't know any other way. It's the banking industry's responsibility to start demonstrating a fair and equitable value proposition for customers, which is in fact transparent. It must do a good job outlining a banking proposition that is understandable for its customers.

But primarily, transparency comes down to an equal value exchange where the information on both sides of the transaction is equal. As mentioned earlier, customers get concerned when they believe that their bank knows something that they don't know and that banks simply take advantage of that in order to create an opportunity to sell something that the customer doesn't really need.

So it's okay to offer a different value proposition to different people, as long as it's clear to each individual person what it is he's getting and how much he's going to pay for it. If banks can articulate that value proposition and do it openly with customers and with regulators, regulators will eventually get onboard. That transparency is actually not uniformity; that non-uniformed banking product and pricing is in the best interest of all of customers.

182

3. No matter what analytic procedures a bank uses, it is still on the hook to avoid discriminatory pricing policies. One of the issues that will not go away in any of the regulatory frameworks, regardless of the geography, is to not price in a way that our regulator feels is discriminatory. Right now what that means is that no matter what a bank's decisions are, what its pricing strategies are, what its product offerings are, it needs to ensure that we're not doing something which accidentally will discriminate a protected class in those areas where that regulatory framework is in place. No matter what the bank does, it'll still be responsible for running those analyses and for making intelligent decisions, which are non-discriminatory.

A classic example of this is in price optimization. People feel that by using information to set a price, which builds on understanding price sensitivity, that this is somehow inherently discriminatory. That is not true. One can show that using price sensitivity just across the dimensions that are already being used for risk-based pricing provides significant uplift and personalization of the experience.

What customers will understand and what banks need to help regulators understand is that by creating personalized products, personalized bundles, personalized pricing, banks are actually doing everyone a favor. And if they could show the regulators that they're not doing this while discriminating against a protected class that will be able to pass regulatory muster.

NOT LETTING BAD THINGS HAPPEN

Obviously the next thing the regulators are concerned about is "bad things happening." What does that mean? Well, there are really two things that regulators and banks should both be concerned about: financial crimes occurring either from another party or from the individual themselves.

So let's talk about third-person financial crime. The biggest issue that's getting a lot of attention these days is international financial crime involving movement of monies across borders— money laundering. The typical regulatory guidelines for Anti-Money Laundering (AML) is to monitor transactions that look unusual. The data and models used to understand how illegal money flows across borders are pretty well understood. There's not much involved in creating a personalized banking relationship that is going to cause additional issues around money laundering. However, as banks apply real-time analytics and next-best-action decision-making technology, they'll be able to use techniques such as Complex Event Processing (CEP) to detect these illegal transactions, just as they do today.

In addition, there's also fraud and theft. Similar data and models are being used to understand and to detect acts of theft and fraud while they're occurring. These models are fairly good at identifying transactions that are unusual, however, more work can be done to integrate information about the individual and how they bank into these models. For example, if the bank analyzes a transaction history, it might find that a credit card was used to purchase an airline ticket to London. If shortly thereafter transactions are occurring in London, it could be useful to take that airline ticket purchase into consideration when defining what transactions are unusual for that particular customer.

There will always be mistakes in these models, and there will always be cases where the bank makes a false positive identification of fraud. As long as information is real-time and pushed out to the user, the bank can actually speed the time for which that transaction is cleared, and the card is put back into circulation.

Not only does this allow the customer a better experience, but it also automates a data-collection process, which is currently manual today, by whitelisting certain types of transactions through an automated push-alert system. The bank is able to add additional transactions into the dataset of what transactions are considered normal.

There's always a concern about first-person fraud. This is when individuals use their own credit and their own account to cause problems. Regulators are concerned that data and models be used to restrict losses due to preventable and predictable circumstances; first-person fraud is one of them.

Again, fraud-detection algorithms and identity-compliance guidelines help prevent the misuse of one's own identity to commit fraud. A personalized banking experience will actually help in gathering additional data and information about the customer in advance. And because the customers' use changes while they are abusing their own identity, these patterns can be detected by banks who are subscribing to data consortium providers who collect identity data and account performance data across a number of different vendors. That will go a long way to reducing concerns from regulators that crimes are being committed inside the bank without the bank's knowledge.

NOT PUTTING THE BANK AT RISK

Of course the biggest focus of regulators over the last several years has been ensuring the stability and liquidity of the banking system. This has been particularly true in the United States and Western Europe where regulators are focused primarily on understanding that a bank can handle the stress of changes to its portfolio.

Given the shift of a bank that's focusing on the individualized and personalized banking experience, this might look like a challenging request. Understanding that each customer is reacting differently and cannot be rolled up to a customer segment or set of products might make this task look difficult to perform.

But let's talk about liquidity. Liquidity is about understanding the asset liability matching process within the bank. Traditionally, asset liability matching happens at the top of the organization where loans and deposits are rolled up into segments and cash flows are matched to make sure there's enough cash on hand to pay depositors when they request their money back and that enough money is flowing in from borrowers to support those requests.

In an individualized banking experience, those individual contracts may look very different from each other, but in order to establish those individualized contracts and to do the data analysis necessary to build that infrastructure, banks have to understand cash flow forecasts at the individual level. So they've actually built the infrastructure behind asset liability matching before they can even offer the products to begin with.

This sounds like a large amount of data, and it is, so banks will need to become much better at large data processing, big data techniques, in order to better understand the cash-flow impact of the behavior of their customers. One of the key tools that has been requested by regulators is the stress test. In a stress-testing project, the regulator asks a bank if it can demonstrate liquidity under very difficult macroeconomic conditions, such as high unemployment or interest-rate shocks.

Right now stress testing is performed as ALM at the top of the organization. What's missing from the analysis is a bottom-up approach by taking each individual contract that's been entered into by the organization, projecting forward new customer contracts based on the data and the analytics that we have performed, and letting that bottom-up forecast essentially meet the top-down forecast in the middle so that differences can be reconciled; when there's a problem with a stress test outcome, it's more likely that the root cause of that problem will be detected in the bottom-up forecast than in the top-down forecast. Those kinds of analytics will make regulators much more comfortable with the results of stress testing.

Finally, a new request from regulators involves model governance. Previously, regulators were mostly interested when models were being used to make decisions at the bank, that these models were preserved, that people understood what they were, and that they were executed uniformly and consistently.

Regulators recently have become much more interested in the statistical and the mathematical process behind each model. This will certainly be the case in all behavioral models used to generate the decisions necessary to create a personalized banking experience. The bank should be prepared to invest in technology that manages models, their construction, and their maintenance. Once a bank moves down the road of using data and analytics to make better decisions, it is a journey that does not end; there will be a need to manage and maintain all of the analytics that are being created for this new banking experience.

As long as the mathematical formulation of the models is consistent with the principles we've spoken about earlier in this book and that documentation is kept about how models are created and maintained, regulators should be comfortable with this information for model governance purposes. This is one of the advantages of employing a system that, as a platform, manages and maintains your analytic assets.

As part of the platform, audit tables and history exist to be able to reconstruct how a particular model was created, the decisions were made in including and excluding certain variables, and a list of all the changes that were made on that model since it first went into production. This is an important element of satisfying the requirement for model governance.

Regulation and Compliance Recap:

Banks do things for three reasons:
1. To make money
2. To save money
3. Because a government told them to

That third category has become an ever-increasing part of the IT budget for banks over the last several years. That trend is likely to continue into the future.

So as banks transform themselves into a more personalized experience that is customer focused, they will still need to be able to answer the questions of regulators. But with appropriate analytics, management, and transparency, a bank should have no problem justifying the decisions they make to regulators.

Clearly, there will always be blocks to making a truly personalized experience because it's forbidden by a particular regulation, but by using a mathematical technique, a decision-making technique such as next best action, these regulatory frameworks can be placed in as constraints to make sure the final output is consistent with what is considered acceptable in your own geographic jurisdiction.

CHAPTER 14. PLANNING THE VISION

What do banks need to do in order to survive? Like anything in nature, an evolution is necessary in order to survive. There are stages that banks need to go through to evolve into an information-based business, one that creates a personalized-value proposition for each customer. There are four major stages of this evolution.

First, banks need to get their own house in order. This means focusing on cleaning up data sources, getting communication between silos organized, and understanding what is actually happening in their business on a day-to-day basis.

Second, they need to improve the products they have today using the data and the information that is so readily available. That comes down to improving existing products.

Third, they need to create new products, new financial services that meet new and changing needs from the marketplace by using the information, the transactional data, and such from the bank that will improve the lives of their customers.

And then finally, in order to truly become an information-based business, banks must leverage the data in the models and turn them outward to the customer to utilize the data and analytics to improve their customers' lives.

GET YOUR "HOUSE IN ORDER"

In order for banks to truly leverage the power of their own data, they need to be able to lower the cost of managing data across the organization. Banks make very short-sighted decisions in data management by keeping data in silos and by not analyzing the data that they have.

There's a lot of talk in the industry about leveraging "big data" to solve problems, but the fact is the banking industry has a "small data" problem. The data that the banks currently have in is not being utilized to its full potential. There are four technologies the banks can use today to actually save money on data management costs. As opposed to creating a centralized data repository, banks can actually create a decision-oriented data store, a data store that has a very specific purpose in mind.

The first technology that is being leveraged today is unstructured data analysis. This is a technique that's being leveraged from the big data space that can be used to save time in mapping different data sets from different parts of the bank into one area. By leveraging unstructured data analysis, we can actually leave the data in the format it is in the source dataset and not have to do conversion work. There are technology companies such as Teradata that are experts in this area; they are making great strides in working with banks to leverage unstructured data analysis to unlock the potential of their data.

Another technology that's helpful is the advent of parallel processing or as some call it, high-performance computing. In parallel processing, the technology leverages multiple computations across a number of different processors at the same time to get a large task done in a shorter period of time. This allows banks to make better decisions by using larger datasets and by running through more and more sophisticated models in a shorter period of time. Companies such as SAS are making great inroads into leveraging parallel processing to help banks build models that they otherwise wouldn't be able to build and to make decisions that they otherwise wouldn't be able to make.

Fuzzy data is a new technology that's being used by banks to improve the decision potential of real-life data that is in the marketplace. For example, today when decisions are made in banks, they are not always made by assuming that the data is absolutely, 100% accurate. It's fairly typical, for example, in originating mortgages in the United States to pull three different credit scores from three different sources and to make a decision with the understanding that some of those credit scores may not be a complete, accurate picture of the person's credit history.

So typically the mortgage underwriter takes the middle score. That's a fuzzy data decision, one based on the understanding that not all of the data is in fact 100% accurate.

Banks don't go through the hassle of trying to reconcile the different credit reports with each other in order to figure out what's missing or what needs to be added in order to get an accurate credit picture. They simply make a decision with the best available information. This is using fuzzy data. It's not a new concept in banking.

IBM is a software company that's making great strides in using fuzzy data. In fact, their Watson hardware and software solution, which is famous for winning the game show Jeopardy, can make decisions in the face of fuzzy data and rank decisions by the percent confidence in the conclusion it's drawing from the data it's reading.

And finally, new technologies are being rolled out in the banking industry to analyze data in place. That would allow a centralized decision-making system to go out to the source data where it exists and pull just the information necessary to make the decision from that source dataset, as opposed to bringing all of the data into one central location, reconciling the differences, and storing it there.

By allowing banks to leave the data where it exists today, it saves us a great deal of the hassle of data extraction and reconciliation projects which require us to physically move and relocate data in a central location.

IMPROVE TODAY

Banks can improve the financial products as they exist today by looking at the entire life cycle as the customer. As customers continue their relationships with the bank, there are five key events. In some sense, they are the only moments that matter.

1. Soliciting the customer by appealing to his need and making sure that the product offers match the individual and who he is.
2. Acquiring that customer with profitable terms and conditions that match the value proposition outline in the marketing phase.
3. Expanding the relationship with the customer by offering additional products and services to expand the share of wallet for that customer.
4. Retaining that customer in the case that the customer decides to move his business to a different institution, or that he no longer needs the financial services. This phase involves finding the correct offer to continue the

relationship in a profitable way for both the customer and the bank.

5. Collecting from that customer in the unfortunate event of having a loan that is no longer performing. That means finding the appropriate offer and strategy by which to maximize cash flow from that customer in a long-term approach.

Most banks are unable to take advantage of these moments that matter, because most of the decisions have three major flaws associated with them. Banks are:

- Too impersonal
- Too late
- Too short sighted

The first mistake that we typically make in the industry is that a bank's decisions are too impersonal. It makes decisions based on broad segments, customer segments involving demographics and psychographics that are static and unchanging. And although on a broad basis this can provide insight into how a customer behaves, it's rarely enough information to make an offer that is relevant and to understand the true individual needs of a customer.

We all know that most of the decisions made across the entire lifecycle of the customer are too impersonal, and therefore when we make those offers the customer feels like the bank doesn't really understand what the customer needs.

The next mistake that banks make is that offers are too late. Because banks have challenges with data and building analytic models that are meant to predict consumer behavior, they've built up an analytic framework that has customer behavior models in the back office in a batch mode, away from the frontline.

What banks know from research is that consumers make decisions based more heavily on information that has been captured in the recent past. And by creating a batch process, analytic process, banks create an information hole and miss the critical elements necessary to predict how a customer will behave because of things that have happened, for example, in the last 24 hours.

For example, banks may have changed their addresses, or moved a significant amount of money into an account, or had a service issue resolved with a branch manager. These are elements that need to be acted on in a fairly short period of time.

As an example, one major bank in the United States analyzed the performance of leads based on traffic on the website. They analyzed the click stream patterns of people coming to gain information about a financial product. Those leads were passed to a call center. Those leads were then processed in order of receipt, which is the common practice.

What this bank learned, however, was that the time that these leads were good was very short, and that if they didn't act on these leads in a very short period of time they were no longer powerful indicators of a buying criteria. And so the bank changed their processing of leads to a last in, first out approach, so that the call center worked on the leads which were newest, rather than the ones that were oldest.

And finally, another mistake that banks make in our decision-making is that our decisions are too short sighted. When they make pricing and retention and collections decisions often times they're looking for short-term profitability gains or a metric that is not aligned with shareholder value at the top of the house, or in lifetime customer profitability. And because they make short-sighted decisions, the banks undercut their ability to build long-term relationships with people and keep their business over a long period of time.

In order for banks to improve today, they need to fix these three problems by creating personalized offers that are real-time in nature, taking information into consideration, which is gathered at the moment that a person is in the front line, interacting with our staff, and finally that maximizes the lifetime customer value.

All three problems, too impersonal, too late, too short sighted, are solved by the three pillars of the personalized bank of the future. By being mobile, the bank fixes the problem of being too late. By having the next best action, the bank fixes the problem of being too impersonal. And by developing truly innovative financial products, the bank fixes the problem of being too short sighted.

Technologies to Improve Today
Of all of the technologies that are available, the one that is most promising to help the industry solve these particular problems is the technology of next best action. Next best action is the use of behavioral modeling and mathematical optimization to find the action of the bank that will maximize the lifetime value of the customer.

This involves two steps. First, the bank needs to measure the impact of their decisions on customer behavior, and in turn, that impact on the lifetime value of the customer. Then taking the bank's goals and limitations into consideration, a mathematical routine is run for each customer that finds the next best action.

This is often confused with a similar technology, next best offer, which is intended to always find the next thing to sell to the customer. But by renaming this technology next best action, the bank recognizes that there are things that it can do to improve the profitability of the customer without necessarily selling them another financial product.

In addition, surveys of customers claim that they do not like to be sold to as often banks would like to sell to them. By taking this into consideration and accepting the desire of customers to have their financial needs met, rather than to always be sold to, banks focus on all sorts of actions including those which may position a new financial product.

This is a relatively emerging technology and a lot of mathematical problems need to be solved in order to truly leverage the benefit of next best action, but a personalized bank, relying on a robust next-best-action technology for each individual customer will serve as the base technology by which services are rendered to customers.

CREATE NEW PRODUCT

Banks need to be proactive in meeting needs of their customers that may have not yet surfaced. Most organizations have a product creation process that they follow in order to successfully generate new products to the market. A five-step approach is often helpful in focusing a team to identify a need and meet it. This approach includes: analysis, ideation, feasibility, design and build, and roll out.

In stage one, a bank looks at the unmet needs of their customers, identifies them, and helps them understand exactly what is behind each need and how they could fulfill it.

In stage two, a bank formulates a team whose job it is to come up with innovative ideas for how to meet those needs. Some of those ideas may not be feasible, but borrowing from agile techniques of small businesses and development teams, a number of different ideas need to be created and tested, which moves us onto phase three.

Each idea needs to be tested for feasibility. There may be some that don't make their way out of the lab because the lack of feasibility is clear, but some need to be tested with customers and tested in the market in order to determine whether that particular idea needs some changing or if it is simply unworkable.

In stage four, the bank engages in a design project that builds that idea and pushes it out into the marketplace. This may require a technological investment or a partnership with another service provider.

And finally, successful new products are rolled out to the marketplace and tested and validated by monitoring customer feedback and assessing the success of the new product in the marketplace.

TURN OUTWARD

Several years ago, Intuit, the financial services software company, did a survey of customers to ask them what would make them switch banking institutions[38]. 52% of those customers indicated that they would switch banking institutions for better advice. The banking industry is often keyed in on the word "advice" as a synonym for investment and retirement planning.

---

[38] "Third Annual Intuit Financial Services Online Financial Management Survey", Intuit Financial Services, October 2010.

But as the survey indicated, that's often not the case with customers. 84% of customer said they would find advice that would help them manage and pay their bills useful. This is a striking contrast to the fairly sophisticated investment and retirement planning advice that we in the banking industry often think of when we think of financial advice.

68% of people said they would find understanding their complete financial picture useful. Such an output seems relatively simple in the age of big data and the power of social media to capture different data sources and put all of that information in one place. But frankly, there are very few places that people can go to get a complete financial picture that doesn't require a great deal of setup work.

66% of consumers said they would find an ability to track their spending useful. This should be an easy one for the banking industry, as we have all of that transaction information available to them. The typical personal financial management (PFM) tools that are available on the marketplace are clearly not meeting the need today. The traction on PFM has not been tracking with expectations from the industry.

This is probably due to the fact that the information is presented in a way that most consumers find foreign to them. The graphing and charting that is a common output for bankers and other financially savvy users has a limited audience appeal. It is up to the banking industry to find an appropriate way to show this information to the customer in a way that will be understandable to them.

44% of customers said that they would find discounts to the stores that they shop in useful. There are a number of banks in the Asia-Pacific region that are experimenting with the use of geolocation-specific offers through a mobile phone. These offers are pushed out to customers when they near a merchant that they have done business with in the past. They are able to get a discount on things that they normally would buy and in turn, by using the debit or credit card of the bank, the bank is able to capture additional interchange revenue from that particular merchant. This kind of win-win needs to be the pattern for the future of banking.

And finally, only 30% of customers said they would find it useful to receive savings advice or additional investment advice. This is the lowest category in the survey and is the one that the industry spends the most of its time and effort in servicing.

Clearly, it is difficult to focus on a mass-market cash flow management product, but that's in fact what customers are saying they want. And the bank's ability to deliver this advice is hampered by thinking that advice needs to be doled out through a branch network in a face-to-face conversation. The future of advice is in interactive, mobile, and personalized data sent directly to our consumers, with a near zero marginal cost.

What is so frustrating in the banking industry is that it has the experts on building models and data and predicting the future of how customers will react. But it keeps this information bottled up behind the wall in its own analytic shops. If banks would simply turn this information outwards to their customers, they would be able to benefit from this great capability that's been built up inside of their institutions.

SEVEN BILLION BANKS

The banking industry has an incredible opportunity ahead of it. Banks can transform what it means to be a bank by creating individual, personalized experiences to each and every customer. Those experiences are so individual that it's almost like a different bank for all seven billion people on the planet.

Banks can achieve this vision by executing on three pillars of the new banking experience:

1. Banking everywhere with a true mobile banking experience
2. Personalized interactions driven by next best action technology
3. A transformed value proposition driven by new, innovative financial products

The banks that can execute on these three concepts will survive. It's just a matter of time before customers and alternative financial services providers will drive the industry to these changes. And as is often the case, the first one there gets a disproportionate share of the benefits.

But the benefits are many. And the future is bright.

I can't wait to meet my personal bank.

ABOUT THE AUTHOR

FRANK H BRIA is a leading authority in using data and analytics to improve the customer experience in retail banking.

Frank started his career using data and analytics in the financial services industry. He has built statistical models for banks including risk, market response, price sensitivity, and customer satisfaction. He has designed and implemented many internal processes at banks around the world to leverage data and analytics in a more intelligent and profitable way.

He has also served as an industry analyst with CEB TowerGroup covering banking analytics where he has spoken at multiple industry conferences on the topic of banking analytics. In addition, he has consulted with banks in North America, Europe, Asia, and Africa on their customer-facing strategies while working with software vendors such as Khimetrics, Response Analytics,
202

and Earnix. He is considered one of the industry pioneers in the use of optimization for pricing retail banking products, having conducted some of the first pilots and implementations in the industry.

Frank resides with his wife and three daughters in Phoenix, Arizona. When he is not traveling to meet with banks and banking vendors to help them plan for the future of the industry, he enjoys the desert outdoors of Arizona often hiking, camping, and hunting. He also has an interest in foreign languages.

Learn more about Frank at FrankBria.com

ONE LAST THING...

If you enjoyed this book or found it useful, I'd be very grateful if you'd post a short review on Amazon. Your support really does make a difference, and I read all the reviews personally so I can get your feedback and make this book even better.

If you'd like to leave a review then all you need to do is click the review link on this book's page on Amazon.

Thanks again for your support!